CORPORATE STRATEGY

MANAGING THE BUSINESS

B. HIRIYAPPA

author<small>HOUSE</small>®

AuthorHouse™ LLC
1663 Liberty Drive
Bloomington, IN 47403
www.authorhouse.com
Phone: 1-800-839-8640

Published by AuthorHouse   11/04/2013

ISBN: 978-1-4918-3117-5 (sc)
ISBN: 978-1-4918-3116-8 (hc)
ISBN: 978-1-4918-3118-2 (e)

Library of Congress Control Number: 2013919869

Contents

Dedicated To

Mother

Preface

Corporate Strategy is an ongoing process in an organization that develops both long-term and short-term objectives at the corporate, business, strategic and operational levels, ready to either establishes and/or modifies the organizational hierarchy to manage operational processes, and determines the values, brand image, sustainability, growth, survival, development, suitability, feasibility and acceptability of the strategy.

In writing this book I have drawn on a vast amount of literature in strategic management. Naturally, I owe an intellectual debt to numerous authors who have enriched in the stream of literature in strategic management by their contributions. My profound debt is for American scholars to George Steiner, Ansoff, Newman, Warren, Peter Drucker, Akcoff, Christenson, Kenneth, Bower and Vacil, Acherman, Robinson, Pierre, Wheeler and Hunger, Porter, Charles W. L. Hill and Gareth R. Jones. In the UK, I owe a great debt to Argeni, Hussey, and Barnard Taylor, Thomson and other scholars. I have taken vast amounts of corporate strategy example from companies such as Apple, Samsung, Microsoft, IBM, Google, Toyota, Tata, Mahindra and others for education and understanding the concept of Corporate Strategy.

Dr. B.HIRIYAPPA. Ph. D.,
drbhiriyappa@gmail.com

CHAPTER 1

INTRODUCTION TO CORPORATE STRATEGY

INTRODUCTION

American and European companies are using different strategies to enter into the emerging market for the expansion of their platform in terms products and services, distribution channels, supply chain management, innovation and technology across the globe to reach ultimate customers. For instance, Wal Mart Stores, Amazon, e-Bay, have been eyeing the emerging retail market. Microsoft, Samsung and Google are prominent players in the international Smartphone market. Multinational corporations are enabling corporate strategies to achieve superiority in products and services, development of the platform, looking for new markets, new customers and innovation of new products and services through strategic partnership, joint venture, mergers and acquisitions, restructuring and turnaround. Corporate strategy is a strategy of an organization. It applies in an organization to achieve and sustain superior performance, to find an organization's challenges and how to be overcoming business challenges. Corporate strategist to find and understanding industry trends, stability, growth, competition, products and services, innovative strength, weakness, opportunities and avoid threats by applying and delivering innovation and enable driving efficiencies in terms of improving profitability, performances. Therefore, an organization bound own corporate strategic department and take responsibility for policy formulation, implementation and control the policy with the help of innovation. It develops system that helps to increase competitiveness and differentiation. It sparks customer spirit and attractive and drives growth of entire business operation in an organization.

Corporate Strategy is an ongoing process in an organization that develops both long-term and short-term objectives at the corporate, business, strategic and operational levels, ready to either establishes and/or modifies the organizational hierarchy to manage operational processes, and determines the values, brand image, sustainability, growth, survival, development, suitability, feasibility and acceptability of the strategy.

Corporate strategy is the design framework of the firm growth and development. Its main objectives is the growth of the company in a particular direction, extent, pace and timing. Corporate strategy involves the objectives design, implementation, control of the objectives of firms which are helpful for growth of company's. It determines the company's mission, vision and long term development and growth of firms. Corporate policy depends on its corporate strategy management. Company Strategist will be framed the appropriate strategy for business operation.

Corporate strategy focuses on resources oriented such as technologies, assets, facilities, skills, management capabilities, approaches. Use these and develop core competencies to achieve superiority of business goals. CEO frame and design corporate strategy to be executing a new platform for promotion of products and services for develop and promote a brand and its image through social network to attractive existed and new customers. The company always builds a core competence platform which focuses on current industry practice and it creates new customers, clients, vendors, and the attractive market for product and services and look for opportunities within the company and outside of the company environment.

Companies are classified into sector wise operation. Sectors are Auto, Bank, Power, Retail, Software, Pharma, Financial, IT, Metal, Oil and Gas, Public Sector Companies, Reality, Tech, Airlines and Services, etc.,.

Retail companies are retail giant Wal Mart Stores, Carrefour, Metro, Tesco, Lidl Stiftung & Co, The Kroger Co, Costco, Aldi, Home Depot, Target Corp.

Airline companies are Qatar Airways, Singapore Airlines, Singapore Airlines, ANA All Nippon Airways, Asiana Airlines, Asiana Airlines, Cathay Pacific Airways, Cathay Pacific Airways, Cathay Pacific Airways, Etihad Airways, Garuda Indonesia, Turkish Airlines, Qantas Airways, Lufthansa, EVA Air, Indian Airline, Indigo, EVA Air, Malaysia Airlines, Swiss Int'l Air Lines and Emirates.

Software companies are Microsoft, Oracle, SAP AG, Symantec Corporation, IBM, TCS, Accenture, Capgemini, Wipro, Mahindra, Infosys, CA Technologies and Adobe, etc.,.

Media companies are Comcast, Google, The Walt Disney Company, Rupert Murdoch's New Corp, Time Warner Inc, Viacom Inc, Sony Entertainment, Bertelsmann SE & Co, Vivendi, Cox Enterprises Inc, Dish Network Corporation, Thomson Reuters Corporation, Rogers Comm, etc.,.

Automobile companies are General Motor, Ford, Tata Motors, Toytoa Motors, Maruthi Suzuki, Hyndai, Mahindra, Fiat, BMW, Audi, SAIC Motors, Volkswagen, Honda, Daimler, Nissan, and Renault etc.,.

Oil and Gas Companies are China Petroleum, Exxon Mobil, Petro China, Chevron, Shell, BP, Petrobras, Ecopetrol, Total, Gazprom, Sinopec, Bharth Petroleum, Indian Oil Corporation, ONGC, Reliance Petroleum, Essar, Cairn etc.,.

FMCG companies are Nestle, Procter & Gamble, Coca Cola, Anheuser—Busch, Philips Morris International, Unilever, PepsiCo, British American Tobacco, Reckitt Benckiser Group, General Mills, Colgate, and ITC etc.,.

Global Mobile Phone companies are Samsung, Nokia now merge with Microsoft, Apple, ZTE, LG, Huawei, TCL, Lenovo and Sony, Blackberry **etc.,.** Smartphone operating systems companies are Taizen and Sailfish, Symbian, Bada, Windows phone, Blackberry, Apple's Ios and Android etc.,.

Pharma and Healthcare companies are Abbott Laboratories, Johnson & Johnson, Pfizer, Hoffmann-La Roche, GlaxoSmithKline, Novartis, Sanofi, AstraZeneca, Abbott Laboratories, Merck & Co, Bayer, Bristol-Myers Squibb, Wyeth, Amgen, Genentech Inc, Daiichi Sankyo, Sinopharm, Merck KGaA, Sun Pharma, Cipla, Dr. Reddy's Lab, Lupin and Cadila etc.,.

Mobile network operators are China mobile, Airtel, Reliance, Vodaphone, Orange, China Unicom, MTN Group, Etisalat, TeliaSonera, Idea Cellular, Tata Teleservices, Aircel and T-Mobile etc.,.

These are the corporate entities and doing business across the world by providing superior quality of services and products with client platform. Strategist determines the future direction of the company and its performance of existing business and will be a future business operation with business and product lines and evaluate how to maximize profitability and optimum utilize of available opportunities for the company.

Corporate strategy department of companies is enabled to observe similar businesses and evaluates available new opportunities that looking for growth. It will happen through strategic alliance for distribution of serving and products and association of using resources, joint ventures with introducing new products and services to new markets and new customer across the globe. The corporate strategy department takes responsibility for the corporate plan and formulating, execute at a functional level, business level and corporate level. It is the prime responsibility of this department. Usually, CEO of the company takes responsibility to overall strategy design responsibility and middle level managers will take responsibility to execute and lower level authority to work to achieve superior goals of the company.

WHAT IS STRATEGY? STRUCTURE OF STRATEGY

IBM is the world's leading management consulting practices. IBM's business strategy expertise can help define and understand market drivers, innovative value propositions, risks, technology strategies, globalization, Mergers and Acquisition activity and the development of new business models. The business strategy offerings help your enterprise understand and leverage core competencies to drive real value by formulating leading-edge, implementable strategies that result in sustainable growth and profitability. Strategy framework is the most responsible and demanding work in companies. Strategist always makes plans for marketing of goods and services for existing, loyal and new customers from across the globe and enhance to provide quality and innovative advance product features facilities to customers.

An organization is able to enable strategic initiatives to do business operation at national and internationally. CEO bound to know the strategy of the company and Strategy structure application in an organization. CEO and team bound to focus on the mission of a company and look for the vision of a company. The CEO must enable business operating model and execute this model to develop a platform for selling products and services to ultimate customers who are widespread across the world. Strategist always monitor the business performance either who comes business or leave the business and find threats and weakness of a company and ready for action plan how to overcome weakness and threats and develop strong strength and make opportunities for a company. Strategy is the future vision of a company.

Corporate strategy useful to the company and more benefited at the time of diversification, it may be over expansion, either over-expansion or too rapid growth, Inadequate financial controls, either Uncontrollable costs or too high costs, Inability to anticipate & deal with new competitors, Inability to anticipate unpredictable shifts in consumer demand and slow or no response to significant external or internal changes.

Corporate performance decline due to recruit an excess number of personnel, Unnecessary and cumbersome administrative procedures, Fear of conflict or taking risks, Tolerating work incompetence at any level or area, Lack of clear vision, mission, or goals, Ineffective or poor communication within various units and between various units.

Apple and Samsung design different business strategies and models within the marketplace and to establish to sell the highly anticipated high end product and services. Apple is to develop and sell new brand, it is innovative products that blended art and technology in order to provide a simple streamline experience to achieve this goal. Meanwhile, Samsung also makes competitive strategy to deliver high end innovative products to achieve its goals. Both companies are offering a bundle of services to customer to capture market share in iPhone segment.

What is the strategy? Is it a plan like short term or long-term? Does it refer to how we will obtain the ends we seek? Is it a position taken any decision? Just like as military forces might take the high ground prior to engaging the enemy; may a business take the position of low-cost provider? On the other hand, does strategy refer to perspective, to the view of the masters, to the purposes, directions, decisions, and actions stemming. Lastly, does strategy refer to a pattern in our decisions and actions? For example, does repeatedly copying a competitor's new product which offerings signal a "me too" strategy? Just what is the strategy?

Strategy is ideas that sustain and grow its business value into the future. The strategy is based on core principles: A CEO finds value, bring specialized expertise in each domain of the business, to make the company as customer driven and make the company be global and establish a strategic competency at market.

A company strategy is to find business challenges, opportunities, drawback, competitive positions, competitors products and services, technology, core platform, market and customers and intellectual resources management and make value creation as branding.

Strategy is all these-it is perspective, position, plan, and pattern. Strategy is the bridge between policy and high-order goals on the one hand and tactics or concrete actions on the other. Strategy and tactics together straddle the gap between ends and means. In short, the strategy is a term that refers to a complex web of thoughts, ideas, insights, experiences, goals, expertise, memories, perceptions, and expectations that provides general guidance for specific actions in pursuit of particular ends. Strategy is at once the course, we chart, the journey, we imagine, and, at the same time, it is the course, we steer, the trip, we actually make. Even when, we are embarking on a voyage of discovery of facts, with no particular destination in mind, the voyage has a purpose, an outcome, and an end to be kept in view.

CONCEPT OF STRATEGY

A strategy is a long-term plan of action. It is designed to achieve a particular superior goal of a company. Strategy applies to many disparate fields such as: Military strategy, strategy, economic strategy, environmental strategy, corporate strategy, business strategy, industry strategy, commerce, science, grand, stability, Expansion, retrenchment, combination, modernization diversification, integration, turnaround, divestment, hybrid, alliance merger and acquisition strategy, etc.,.

Strategy is essentially linked with military science. It implies facing the enemy under war conditions that are to one's advantage. A policy when given a particular meaning under a prevailing situation and in view of the enemy or competitor policy becomes a strategy. So, **strategy can be defined as interpretative planning. Strategy includes the determination and evaluation of alternative paths to an already established mission or objectives, and eventually choosing the right alternatives, In common sense, a strategy outlines how management decides and plans to achieve its goal and objectives.** Management formulates strategy to shade out the effect of other polices of it's out the overall plan and program's of the competitors, policy to avail of competitive advantage.

COMPANY / CORPORATE STRATEGY

Corporate strategy is the expression of the current hypothesis for what the corporation should be doing. It is, inevitably, a hypothesis, because we cannot get absolute data about matters like customer needs; competitor's plans; the future state of the economy, A company strategy concerns with core values in terms of innovation, excellent customer services and social responsibility, core purposes concerns with updated and new technology, visionary goals are profit, competitive advantages, capturing market share, long term sustains and development and growth, business vision. It is the long term direction of the companies to achieve sustainable development, development platform to sell products and services by using innovative technologies and grab market share by introducing new feature products and services customers across the globe.

McKinsey's Corporate Strategy as "**Developing a strategic direction, supported by the necessary reallocation of resources and coordinated business unit plans, and designing a sustainable strategy development process**'.

GM's Corporate Strategy as "GM are Focused on a single global vision: To design, build and sell the world's best vehicles. This powers the development of world class products that are winning in the marketplace, and is helping to transform our business and fortify our balance sheet".

The Corporate Strategy exposes identify to the numerous methods that businesses use to create competitive advantage in their marketplace. Consultant learn how to evaluate the competitive implications of broader trends, analyze competitors, identify growth opportunities, and create successful brands. The Corporate Strategy helps to properly approach a vast array of business situations ranging from challenges with starting a new firm with growing revenue in a mature business.

Samsung corporate strategy is different from Apple, Just a few years back, Samsung struggle to capture the Smartphone market.

Today capture Smartphone market to apply of corporate strategy. Apple is the world's largest technology company by revenue. Samsung hyped to launch of Galaxy S4 Smartphone, it is the latest step as it tries to overtake Apple, due to a massive and impressive new features. In the same way, Apple launched 5c Smartphone and able to capture the market from Samsung with a rivalry of Microsoft and Google.

Core pillars of Samsung Corporate strategy as outlined:

"Learning from Competitors strategies, products, business lines, product lines, a service line of attracting customers and innovation of new Smartphone. The concentration of research and development to launch and produce Smartphone across the globe, it brings a combination of a phone / tablet, it made hit for Samsung in International market. Samsung is a diverse business with chips, displays, and other technology. It used massive advertising policy for promoting flagship Galaxy phones. Samsung having well supply chain and distribution, it is also corporate advantage. Low cost of Smartphone, it considers past things and make well in future strong capable leader in a Smartphone".

American Global computing software giant Microsoft aggressive and a massive strategic reorganization to try to compete with its two biggest rivals, Apple and Google. Microsoft-Nokia deal is likely to promote growth and competition in the under-penetrated Smartphone space in India, and could lead to potential price cuts in Smartphones—the Lumia series uses Windows 8 system but will no longer be required to pay licensing fee—and quasi-Smartphones like the Asha series, thanks to cost synergies from licensing, patents, intellectual property and R&D capabilities. Microsoft and nokia deal would make revolutionize the mobile market in emerging markets with aggressive competing strategies with Apple and Google.

Corporate strategy is enabling the company strategy. It is integrated growth, profitability, and socio-environmental responsibility is keywords in our corporate strategy. It helps to corporate Strategy department to make and take the right decisions to allow them to take advantage of opportunities while minimizing risks. Combining world-class industry research with decades of hands-on experience, Any company Corporate Strategy activities include that build targeted customer, growth and channel strategies, define a corporate vision linked to tangible actions and goals, improve operational performance, engage in strategic performance measurement and management, conduct market, competitive and industry analysis, design organizational structures and allocate resources, a company strategy is the game plan management, It can be used to stake out market position, company strategy is a long-range blueprint of an organization's desired image, direction and destination what it wants to be, what it wants to do and where it wants to go.

Google is one of technology companies and is a search giant, and it is also performing extremely well in the advertising, mobile, and cloud-based spaces and going up against competitors such as Microsoft and Apple.

- It consciously considered and flexible designed long term plan and intent to achieve goals for this purpose to mobilize resources, to direct effort and behavior, to handle events and problems, to perceive and utilize opportunities, and to meet challenges and find threats to corporate survival and success.
- It will be conducted operations in terms of attracting and please to customers.
- It will be completed successfully in competitive markets.
- Its achieve company goals and objectives.
- The company's strategy consists of the combination of competitive moves and business approaches that managers employ to please customers compete successfully and achieve organizational objectives.

Strategy, then, has no existence apart from the ends sought. A general framework provides guidance for actions to be taken and, at the same time, which is shaped by the actions taken. This means that the necessary precondition for formulating strategy is a clear and widespread understanding of the ends to be obtained. Without these ends in view, action is purely tactical and can quickly degenerate into nothing more than a flailing about.

When there are no "ends in view" for the organization with large, strategies still exist and they are still operational, even highly effective, but for an individual or unit, not for the organization as a whole. The risks of not having a set of company-wide ends clearly in view include missed opportunities, fragmented and wasted effort, working at cross purposes, and internecine warfare. A comment from **Lionel Urwick's classic *Harvard Business Review*** article regarding the span of control is applicable here listed below:

> **"There is nothing which rots morale more quickly and more completely than . . . The feeling that those in authority do not know their own minds."**

For the leadership of an organization to remain unclear or to vacillate regarding ends, strategy, tactics, and the means is to not know their own minds. The accompanying loss of morale is enormous.

One possible outcome of such a state of affairs is the emergence of a new dominant coalition within the existing authority structure of the enterprise; one that will augment established authority in articulating the ends toward which the company will strive. Also possible is the weakening of authority and the eventual collapse of the formal organization. No amount of strategizing or strategic planning will compensate for the absence of a clear and widespread understanding of the ends sought.

SAS corporate strategy as **"define, plan, execute and validate strategies and goals by providing data integration, model development, reporting, collaboration and analysis tools with role-based security.** SAS is the leader in business analytics software and services, and the largest independent vendor in the business intelligence market. Through innovative solutions delivered within an integrated framework and helps customers. SAS is recognised by the IT analyst community as a visionary in performance management—particularly when it comes to advanced analytical approaches, strategy management, cost and profitability optimization.

CHARACTERISTICS OF CORPORATE STRATEGY

Corporate strategist always understands customers, competitors and costs, target the customers, segment the market, gain competitive advantages, better supply chain, adapt innovative technology, use social network for marketing of products and services to client and sustain value and develop a brand image and maximize the profitability and maximize intellectual property and establish superior performance towards to reach the vision and mission of a corporation. A corporate strategy has the following characteristics.

- It is long range planning, apart from also consider and cope with the short term planning.
- Strategies are specific actions suggested achieving the objectives.
- Strategies are action oriented.
- It can be formulated at the top level management and delegate and associate powers to middle level and low level for policy formulation, implementation and control of strategy.
- It copes with a competitive and complex setting in corporate environment.
- Its goals and objectives are translates them into reality in corporate.
- It concerns with perceiving opportunities and deployment of resources and threats and seizing initiatives to cope with them
- Everyone is empowered to implement the strategy.
- Strategies are means to an end.
- Strategies are concerned with uncertainties with competitive situations like risk etc., which are likely to take place at a future date.

- Strategy is deployed to mobilize the available resources in the best interest of the company.
- It gives special importance to the combination, sequence, timing, direction and depth of various moves and action initiatives taken by managers to handle environment uncertainties and complexities.
- It is flexible and dynamic.
- It provides unified criteria for managers in function of decision making in corporate.
- It is multi-prolonged and integrated with the objectives and goals of corporate . . .
- Corporate strategy is a proprietary set of actions that enables a company to be worth more than just the sum of its parts. The most critical role of the center is to enable its business unit strategies to achieve leadership positions. The center adds differential value to its business units in four areas: providing a compelling corporate vision and appropriate performance objectives, aggressively managing the portfolio, leveraging a repeatable operating model and executing a balanced financial strategy.

NATURE, SCOPE AND CONCERNS OF CORPORATE STRATEGY

Corporate strategy is the direction to an organization about Buildup value for company strategies and superior objectives, vision, mission and goals with value, right to make resource allocation and planning, develop dedicating resources to develop required capabilities and harvest capital from unproductive uses, to make appropriate compensation, effective performance management, efficiency in managing operational execution, create value communication, always reinforcing key value messages. Corporate strategy is to find markets, competition, industry changes, adapting business models, and mergers, acquisitions and divestitures. Corporate strategy concerns with continuing as is business operation, acquire a competitor, develop up regional office, develop new products for the current market and current product, penetrate more into existing markets and maintain reposition.

Corporate strategy is basically concerned with the choice of businesses, products and markets of the company's. Nature, scope and concerns of corporate strategy as outlined below:

* ❖ It can be involved and viewed with objectives designed framework strategy of the firm.
* ❖ A strategy designed framework is filling the firm's strategic planning gap.
* ❖ Leverage core competencies to formulate innovative strategies, create new business models and ensure successful transformations for sustainable growth and profitability.
* ❖ Actually, it is concerned with the different choice of the firm's products and markets. It generally involves the changes/ additions / deletions in the firm's existing product market positions in businesses. It serves the customers needs and requirements and meets and serves the business requirement.
* ❖ It's able to ensure that the right fit to businesses and how to achieve between the firm's and its business environment.
* ❖ It helps and focuses to build up the relevant competitive advantages for the firm's in the market.
* ❖ Both corporate objectives and corporate strategy bring together and describe the firm's business concepts.
* ❖ It will monitor developments to ensure that they are running smoothly.
* ❖ It will evaluate the strategy and challenge each department head or specific employees within departments on how the strategy is being executed.
* ❖ It is to actually execute the strategy.
* ❖ The strategy department always has some input into the process of buying or divesting companies. It prepares analysis of potential target firms and evaluates whether it coincides with the firm's overall strategy. In addition, the department may recommend that one division is not performing well and

should be sold off. It may also recommend that a division does not fit in with the overall strategic direction of the firm or does not bring any economies of scale so it can be divested.

CORPORATE STRATEGIC OBJECTIVES

Corporate Strategic objectives would include targets for sales revenue, profit, return on investment, growth, market share, shareholder value and corporate image and reputation, superior efficiency in services, Quality of products and services at low cost, resource allocation and planning, performance management, value communication, development of intellectual property, innovation, well research skilled persons to manage business operations.

❖ Corporate strategies are providing direction to company CEO is to make plans and enable to enter new economic markets. It specifies goals that are closely associated future sustainability, value creation, development of brand image, enhance to market share, customers, superior supply chain, balance score of entire company's operation.

❖ Core competencies include good customer service, unique products that are difficult for competitors to duplicate and the use of a supply chain to deliver products into the economic market.

❖ Business strategies help companies create a competitive advantage in the marketplace. Corporate, department and business-level strategies are commonly used by business owners to create a competitive advantage. Corporate strategies provide direction when the company enters new economic markets. Department strategies outline specific goals for individual business departments. Business-level strategies focus on a specific function that can increase a company's market share and profitability. These strategies also integrate various economic resources to improve a company's production efficiency.

WHAT DOES CORPORATE STRATEGY ENSURE IN FIRM'S BUSINESSES

Any company Corporate Strategy continuously changes the business mix toward higher value, more profitable technologies and looking for market opportunities across the globe. A company looking and become a globally integrated enterprise to capture new customer, new technology, new market, new innovative products: it results that growth and sustainable development. A company always meets clients' needs and requirement and make company become financially strong and to invest in future sources of income, growth and provide strong returns to shareholders. A company focuses to deliver long-term value and performance to achieve superior objectives and goals. A long-term perspective ensures Apple, Samsung, IBM, Google and Microsoft companies are well positioned to take advantage of major shifts occurring in technology, business and the global economy. These companies also galvanizes to deliver superior performance in terms of quality products and services to ultimate clients.

* ❖ Corporate strategy first time ensure that the firm's business growth and correct alignment of the firm's and its environment.
* ❖ It primarily ensures that enhancement new and updated technology and opportunities are converted into competitive advantages to the company. It leads to enhance core competency for products, customers, suppliers, distributors, and stakeholders of a firm.
* ❖ It's ready to serve and ensure that the design strategy which for filling the strategic gaps in business.
* ❖ It helps and serves to build up the firm's relevant competitive advantages,
* ❖ It ensures to establish superiority in performance, delivery and maintain and provide value base services to clients.
* ❖ Its primary strategy ensures that the masterminding and working out the right opportunity which fit between the firm and its external environment.

- ❖ It enable to find innovative products and services to gain to access to vast, new, existing market share and providing advanced features included in products and services to develop a competitive advantage for a company.
- ❖ It helps to establish strategic partnerships, joint venture, mergers with competitors, clients, and similar industries. It makes as market leader in a particular business operation.
- ❖ Corporate strategy purposefully firm's weakness converts into strengths and threats converts into opportunities in this way ensure to firm's businesses.
- ❖ It enable to find client platform and development platform to sell products and services into different segment to across the globe.
- ❖ It ensures that responding the environment is part and parcel of a firm's existence in the market.
- ❖ It find and make wherever necessary to restructure the organization, turnaround and liquidate to business operation.
- ❖ It ensures to arise a major question which is better and how to methodical to response to firm's.
- ❖ Corporate strategy is the opposite of ad hoc responses to the changes in the environment in competition, consumer tastes, technology and other variables in firms.
- ❖ It definitely involves the amounts is to long-term, well thought out and prepared responses to the various forces in the business environment.
- ❖ It able to find and ensures that heavy income spend in research and development and bring innovative products and services at low cost.

STRATEGY IS PARTLY PROACTIVE AND PARTLY REACTIVE

The company strength's strategy is typically a blend in the following circumstances:

1) Proactive actions on the part of managers and responsibility to improve the company's market position, technical upgradation,

develops intellectual property and skills persons and financial performance.

2) It will be needed reactions to be unanticipated developments in new market, new customers, social network to promote services to clients, innovative products and services and fresh market competitive conditions in the firm's businesses.

The biggest portion of the company's current strategy flows from previously initiated actions like experiences, resources, strengths, technology and competitive capabilities along with business approaches. These are working well enough to merit continuation and newly launched managerial initiatives to strengthen the overall position and performance in terms of growth rate and market share of firm's. These things are involved in management game plans. It is deliberate and proactive. It is standing the product of firm's product and services management analysis and strategic thinking determine about the company's situation analysis and its conclusion about how to position the company in the marketplace and how to tackle the task of compositing for buyer patronage.

Figure—1.1: A Company's Actual Strategy Is Partly Planned and Partly Reactive

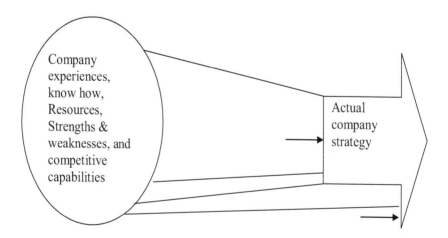

In this figure clearly indicates the every strategic movie is not the result of proactive plotting and deliberate management design. Things are happening in a company which cannot be fully anticipated or planned in companies. When the market and competitive conditions of the company will take either unexpected turn or some aspect of a company's strategy hits stone wall. Some kind of strategic reaction or adjustment is required for companies. Therefore, a portion of the company's strategy is always developing the project. It is coming as a reasoned response to unforeseen developments in the form of fresh strategic maneuvers on the part of rival firms in the market. These are shifting customer requirements and expectations to new technologies and market opportunities which are suitable to be changing political or economic climate or other unpredictable or unanticipated happenings in the surrounding environment. But apart from adapting the strategy which has to changes in the market. And also a need to adapt strategy in terms of new learning emerges. It is pieces of the strategies which are working well with firm and which aren't and as management hits upon new ideas for improving the strategy. Crafting a strategy involves stitching together either a proactive or intended strategy and then adapting first one piece and then another as circumstances that surrounding the company's situation change or better options to emerge as a reactive / adaptive strategy.

DEALING WITH STRATEGIC UNCERTAINTY

❖ Strategic uncertainty is representative of the future uncertain trend or event which has unpredictable in real business.
❖ Information gathering and additional analysis in companies will not able to reduce the uncertainty
❖ Scenario analysis is basically acceptable uncertainty in business. The scenario can be used driven description of two or more future scenarios.
❖ Each uncertain require a suitable strategy to make into certainty in the company's business.

❖ Strategic uncertainty is the strategic implications of strategic managers.

❖ It is a key construct in strategy formulation.

❖ External analysis will be emerged with so many of strategic uncertainties to company's.

❖ Uncertainties can be managed; these can be grouped into logical clusters or themes.

❖ Strategic uncertainty is useful and assesses the importance of each cluster in order to set problems with regard to relevant and appropriate information gathering and analysis.

❖ Suitable strategic decisions help to strategist in gathering information, analysis of uncertainties in businesses.

❖ Changing conditions of uncertainty, strategist can form a suitable strategy for changing the context of uncertainty of business.

IMPLICATIONS OF STRATEGIC UNCERTAINTY

❖ Each strategic uncertainty involves potential trends or event which can be impacted on present, proposed and even potential strategic business units of company's.

❖ Impact of strategic uncertainty will be depended on the strategic business unit of a firm.

❖ Some of strategic business units in a firm which more important to compare to other units in strategic business units.

❖ Established strategic business units may be indicated in terms of associated of sales, profits and costs of products and services.

❖ Sales, profits and cost of products and services may not reflect the true value of a firm.

❖ Information needed areas are affected several strategic business units of company's.

❖ Strategic uncertainty implications are to be relevant to impact on strategic uncertainty.

CHAPTER 2

DEVELOPMENT OF CORPORATE STRATEGY

INTRODUCTION

Any company will work for prolonged for development of strategy that turn into an emerging strategy for global market. A strategist will focus on development of social network, value, brand building, product lines, new market, new customer, added innovative services, superior customer services, effective supply chain management, improvement of performance, retain the talented human resources, develop skills learning, training and development programs for employees, clients, customers, retain existing, new and loyal customers and brings continuous improvement in terms of performance, quality of products and services and ready to update changes in a company. A corporate strategic team will take responsibility and enables to develop a strategy before introducing any innovative products and services to market. Strategist always effectively utilizes social network for development of brand, values, social responsibility of a company and its highlights products innovative features message must reach to ultimate customers. These are key and the prime responsibility of a strategic group of a any corporate. All these activities will lead to get the order from clients before introducing products, services and also get customer feedback in the form of recommendations, suggestions for how to be improvement of product features and platform for marketing of innovative goods and services to ultimate customers.

Established Nokia is failure due to lost its competitive advantage with other mobile companies such as Apple, Samsung and Google. A gigantic software company Microsoft acquired Nokia and restructuring its mobile Smartphone operation in emerging markets especially India and China and Smartphone operation across the globe. The company either success or failure purely depends on policy matter of a company, how its formulation, implement, and what manner curb internal and external environment weakness and threats and overall, controlling, monitoring and managing processes of operation. Strategic department's failure due to be making long term future oriented strategies of the company and unable to develop an innovative technology, platform skills, and advance learning platform, reducing the research and development budget, lost the competitive advantage, unable to update mega advance feature development use for introducing new products and services. All these factors are identified by a company when the market is shifted, Clients are not interested about technology, products, services, values and performance. So that it is the best time for to re-evaluate CEO entire company actions into benefits side structure and strategic department enable too working for designing innovative corporate strategy. This strategy bound to overcome all firing issues that are concerning for failure of long term objectives and goals of a company.

A company enables its Corporate Strategy by knowing the facts such as today's organization position, status, culture, clients, products and services, core competency platform, marketing social network platform, future technology, committed skilled and advance learners, values and performance superior in performance to clients, distributors, suppliers, customers and stakeholders of the company. CEO is to know, Where an organization is today, where want it to be and how want to get there in the future. Corporate strategies enable corporate strategic plan and it enables to clients and the general public. It is the process of a company: it should determine how a company will be organized, set objectives, define policies and allocate resources, operate on a day-to-day basis. Development of corporate **strategic approach serves as a framework for strategic, exploration, decision making, commitment, action, and learning. A strategic group will be taken to be learned measures and adapts the strategic management process in real time by utilizing key performance indicators. Overall,** It is the process of finding values, vision and mission of a company, to work under corporate healthy culture, and maintain global delivery network and attract, develop, and retain the best talent and introduce innovative products and services and fulfill customer requirements.

The majority of the case, strategic planning involves starting with a problem, analyzing the root cause of the problem, developing solutions to the problem, and then formulating a set of initiatives to address the problem. This approach can work for many organizations, but it will not result, in a state of positive deviant performance—the achievement of extraordinary success beyond the expectations of both stakeholders and outside observers. Strategic team looks for internal environmental analysis: it is to find the strengths and weakness of a company and external environment analysis is to find opportunities and threats of a company. Competitive advantages analysis is to enable to sell company products through effective management of distribution channels at local market and international market.

The strategy formulation approach serves as a framework for strategic exploration, decision making, commitment, action, and learning. Strategic manager considers industry driver impact such as new entrants, new substitutes, new market, merger, and acquisitions activities, shifting business.

THE STAGES OF CORPORATE STRATEGY FORMULATION— IMPLEMENTATION PROCESS

Development of corporate strategy, is the responsibility of the CEO and strategic group of a company. It will prolong to define strategy for a company. A company's management will know well the strengths, opportunities, weakness and threats for corporate level, business level and functional level, to make list priorities, choices, how to accomplish superior goals of a company, what are the corrective actions will be used at the time constraints raised and to how overcome constraints. Development of the corporate strategy is the main objective of the company. It is the process of combining all activities of the various functional areas of a business and able to achieve its vision and mission of a company. Craft and executing strategy are the heart and soul of managing a business enterprise. The formulation of corporate strategy is a subject which does not lend itself to a generic approach which can be copied and tailored to fit. Corporate strategy formulation is the future vision based strategic planning. It involves a situation assessment that establishes a shared assessment of the current and future situation among the senior directors, strategist and the client team. **The strategy developer of company bound to define strategic options and specifies strategic initiatives which create significant value for the business, company operations and clients.**

Fortune 500 companies are given prominent time for development of strategy for development, survival, growth and buildup values, social responsibility and enhance to launch new advance feature and technology updated quality products and services at low cost and continuous improvement of services.

Strategist always finds core competence of a company and its products, services and develop plans for how to sell company's products at local and international market and analysis of existing companies products and services available in the domestic and international market and find who are the competitor and product, price, quality, promotes differentiation strategy in the market to achieve superior performance and goals.

The company either success or failure depends on the strategy of the company and its CEO is responsible for the strategy development, implement and control and curb unnecessary activities that are not directly or indirectly associated with business operation across the globe.

Crafting and executing a company formulation's strategy **is divided into five steps as outlined:**

Figure—2:1: the stages of corporate strategy formulation—implementation process

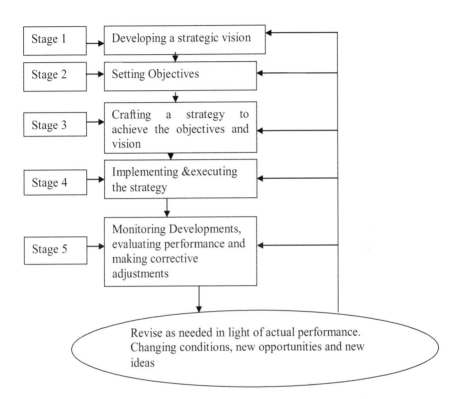

Figure 2.1 indicates the stages of corporate strategy formulation implementation process are listed below:

1) Developing a strategic vision as concerned with company's future products and services platform which based on customer-market-technology.
2) Setting objectives and using them as a yardstick for measurement the company's performance and progress relating to present and future.
3) Crafting a strategy to achieve the desired outcomes and move the company along with the strategic discipline which management has charted.

4) Implementation and executing the selected strategy efficiently and effectively discharge in the company.

5) Monitoring, developments and initiating corrective adjustments towards the company's long term direction, objectives. Strategy or execution in light of the company's actual performance.

STAGE 1: DEVELOPING A STRATEGIC VISION

CEO, Managing Board, team of strategist has taken responsibility for developing a **vision statement of a company. This team sets questions and makes answer themselves, and define the progressive definition of** a vision of a company:

❖ What do we want to do going forward?
❖ When do we want to do it?
❖ How do we want to do it?

Nanus defines a vision as a realistic, credible, attractive future for [an] organization. It is related to the future and lifeline of an organization

Harari defines as **"Vision should describe a set of ideals and priorities, a picture of the future, a sense of what makes the company special and unique, a core set of principles that the company stands for, and a broad set of compelling criteria that will help define organizational success."**

Strategic Vision of Microsoft as **"Global diversity and inclusion is an integral and inherent part of our culture, fueling our business growth while allowing us to attract, develop, and retain this best talent, to be more innovative in the products and services we develop, in the way we solve problems, and in the way we serve the needs of an increasingly global and diverse customer and partner base".**

Apple's Vision Statement

"Apple is committed to bringing the best personal computing experience to students, educators, creative professionals and consumers around the world through its innovative hardware, software and Internet offerings."

Samsung Vision statement of Samsung Vision 2020

Samsung Electronics' vision for the new decade is to "Inspire the World, Create the Future."

We are committed to inspiring communities around the world by developing new technologies, innovative products and creative solutions. We are also committed to creating a brighter future by developing new value for our core networks: industry, partners and employees. Through these efforts, we hope to contribute to a better world and a richer experience for all. As part of our new vision, we have mapped out a specific plan of reaching $400 billion in revenue and becoming one of the world's top five brands by 2020. To this end, we have also established three strategic approaches in our management: creativity, partnership and talent.

We are excited about the future. As we build on our previous accomplishments, we look forward to exploring new territories, including health, medicine and biotechnology. We are committed to being a creative leader in new markets and becoming a truly No. 1 business going forward.

Role of Apple's Vision Statement

Apple's Vision statement clearly states their long-term goals for the future. They are committed to bringing the best computing and learning experiences to consumers and through their continuous

research and launch of new products they are able to give their target markets what they want. Apple's vision is to become the "best" at designing and manufacturing electronic devices in the world. They set their quality standards high using the word "best" and so far they have yet to fail. Their vision is a promise to the consumers. They are "committed" in producing high quality products and providing high quality service thus setting high industry standards for other competitors.

Microsoft, Apple, Samsung and others company vision statement highlights and notices to following things to the CEO and Strategic initiative team at the time of defining a vision statement: Company's strategic team know and understand a useful strategic vision statement is a thorough description of the future state of the company;

- It's bound to clarity of the long term nature and future platform of a company.
- It's bound to define an innovative platform for new technology, products, services, market, clients, supplier, vendor, human resources, corporate culture and advance learning skills and retain talent.
- It specify time schedule for achieving superior performance development, objectives and goals of a company.
- Its concern with long term sustainability and development, growth, profitability and value creation and create brand reputation and a company image.
- ❖ It paints a picture in words and numbers of what the business will be at a certain point in time in the future. It includes a measurable summary financial target which, when attained, assures strategic success by generating sufficient economic value for the company to remain a desirable business entity (compared to what investors could achieve by investing in something else).
- ❖ Strategic vision is the future of the company's products, services, market, customer and technology. These are focused to improve its current market position and its future prospect.

❖ It must be determined the proper directional path the company and should take changes in the company's product and services.

❖ Strategic manager in company carefully draw and reasoned to make conclusions about how to try to modify the company's business and market position in business.

❖ Top management's views and conclusions about the company's attribute towards the products, services, customer, market and technology, these are focusing and constitute a strategic vision for the company.

❖ A strategic vision defines management aims and aspirations for the business and points an organizing in a particular direction path towards the strategic path for identifying the current trends and estimation of the future trends towards the company's business.

❖ Well and Clear defined strategic vision ready to communicates management's aspirations to stakeholders and it helps to guide and encourage energies of company personnel in a common direction.

❖ **Develop consensus strategic vision and it look for markets, products, industry value chain and financial structure and to find a basis of competition from competing.**

Mission and Strategic Intents

Mission and strategic intents indicate the ongoing activities of a company. It focuses the what a company is doing day to day activities and it covers the complete area of operation and its use of strategies. Mission is to enable the short term direction of the company to achieve superior performance, value creation, develop a short plan for selling the products and services and expansion of market through diversification of business, joint venture and strategic alliances. CEO takes responsibility for formulating policy relating to day to day operation of business and achieve to expansion of core competencies and take strategic competitive advantages to manufacture products and services and effective value chain performance, able to compete with competitor in national and international market with similar products and services.

❖ Strategic managers should be clearly know about their role and responsibilities to company, these are expressed in terms of statement of mission.

❖ Mission and strategic intents are very important both external stakeholders and others managers in the company's.

❖ Mission statements clearly defined and it should accomplish by strategic managers in firms.

❖ Mission statements intents is not concerned with the details of strategic business unit competitive strategy or the directions and methods the businesses, it will be taken to achieve a complete position rather, the concern of firm's overall directional strategic decision.

❖ Communication builds understanding, develops consensus, and encourages commitment.

Strategic managers of a subsidiary will be responsible for changing and developing a strategy for business. While definitions of strategy should be clear and it fit into the firm's subsidiary business and the entire group.

Hamel and Prahalad have highlighted the importance of clear strategic intent can go much further in the business and activities are listed below:

❖ It can be provided with motivation and galvanize along with enthusiasm throughout the organization

❖ It is providing what they call a sense of density and discovery in business.

❖ When the absence of these, there is risk of different parts of the organization in terms of different levels of management, all members of the organization, it should be pulling in different directions in the firm's activities.

Decisions are a major part of the overall mission in a major corporation, it will exercise constraints elsewhere in business activities. The corporation aspires to earn short-term profits or long-term growth; its focus on selected countries corporation ready to make investment particularly in internal innovation use and develop the new products, or the acquisition of the other businesses. For this purpose, to develop strategic choice with regard to strategic matter explicit and it can help to make strategic decisions.

Stage 2: Setting Objectives

Finland base Nokia was setting objectives for long term sustainability and introducing new mobile phones to emerging market and a global. Today, Nokia objectives are a failure due to heavy loss and unable to use new Smartphone platform and unable to get a competitive advantage. Nokia is unable to compete with Samsung, Apple and Google. Therefore, it is merged with software giant Microsoft and Microsoft sets new objectives for promotion of Smartphone platform development and its customer base and product features. A company is **setting goals and objectives crucial but it is the first and most critical step in a company's planning process. Objectives are the desired results of an individual or an organization envisions, plans and commits to achieve—key to control and strategy of the company.**

It demands a yardstick to measure, specific, appropriate realistic, timely objectives of a company. When an objective lacks in measurable, specific, appropriate, realistic and timely, it is not very useful. Most of strategic objectives are directed toward improvement maximizing profits and higher returns to the shareholders and useful to stakeholders of a company.

Setting objectives play a magnificent role in development and designing of the company mission and vision. Basically, they represent the quantum of growth in this way seeks and achieve in the given time frame. It also endows the company features, products, services, and its characteristics that ensures the projected the growth. Objectives are setting the process, and also tackling the environment and deciding to appropriate objectives in business. Objectives main aim is to be **mobilized, utilizes, preparation and planning for resources and greatly increase the odds of success and timely project completion.**

❖ The objectives provide the basis for major decisions of the firm and also said the organizational performance to be realized at each level.

❖ The main purpose of the setting objectives is to convert the strategic vision into specific performance targets such as results and outcomes of the management in the company.

❖ Setting objectives are yardsticks for tracking the company's progress and performance.

❖ Setting objectives is the specific tool for truly stretching an organization to reach its full potential core capabilities.

❖ Company objectives should be improving the financial positions, economic positions and business positions.

❖ Company objectives are to be more intentional and focused on actions.

❖ The objectives are short term and long term objectives which are supported for business enterprise.

They help to channel employees throughout the organization toward common goals. This helps to concentrate and conserve valuable resources in the organization and to work collectively in a more timely manner.

Second, challenging objectives can help to motivate and inspire employees throughout the organization to higher levels of commitment and effort. A great deal of research has supported the notion that individuals work harder when they are striving toward specific goals instead of being asked simply to "do their best".

Third, there is always the potential for different parts of an organization to pursue their own goals rather than overall company goals. Although well intentioned, these may work at cross purposes to the organization as a whole. Meaningful objectives thus help to resolve conflicts when they arise. Finally, proper objectives provide a yardstick for rewards and incentives. Not only will they lead to higher levels of motivation to employees but also they will help to ensure a greater sense of equity or fairness when rewards are allocated.

The Balanced Scorecard Approach

The Balanced Scorecard Approach developed by Robert Kaplan and David Norton in 1992. It consists of four **Perspectives** and to develop metrics, collect data and analyze, it's relative to each of these perspectives: **The Learning & Growth Perspective, The Business Process Perspective, The Customer Perspective, The Financial Perspective.** It is to develop metrics, collect data and analyze it relative to each of these perspectives. The balanced scorecard is a management system (not only a measurement system) that enables organizations to clarify their vision and strategy and translate them into action. It provides feedback around both the internal business processes and external outcomes in order to continuously improve strategic performance and results. When fully deployed, the balanced scorecard transforms strategic planning from an academic exercise into the nerve center of an enterprise.

❖ It is a combination of strategic and financial objectives of the company.

❖ It measures the company performance for this purpose, it is required for setting both types of financial and strategic objectives and tracking their achievement.

❖ The strategic manager takes more care and design the strategic objectives than on achieving financial objectives in business.

The Balanced Scorecard Approach is a popular approach. The majority of Fortune 1000 companies are using this methodology for developing metrics, collect data and analyze data.

STAGE 3: CRAFTING A STRATEGY TO ACHIEVE THE OBJECTIVES AND VISION

Strategy Making is the complex task of the CEO and Strategic group of a company. It addresses a series of strategic how's will do to achieve set objectives and goals, to b Requires choosing among strategic alternatives, to Promotes actions to do things differently from competitors rather than running with the herd and it is a collaborative team effort that involves managers in various positions at all organizational levels.

Crafting a strategy to achieve the objectives and vision is the third stages corporate strategic process in strategic management.

❖ A company's strategy is at full power only when it's processed from the corporate level to the business level and then from the business level to the functional level and operating levels in firms.

❖ Middle level and Frontline managers cannot do good strategy making without understanding the company's long-term direction and higher level strategies apart from the vision and mission of the company.

❖ Strategy makers in a company belong to the same team and involved in many different pieces of the overall strategy crafted at various organizational levels that need to be in sync and united.

❖ Achieving the unity is the basic tools in strategy making and it is partly a function of communicating the company's basic strategy, this theme effectively across the whole organization and establishing clear strategic principles and guidelines for lower level strategy that helpful in making strategy at lower levels in the company.

❖ Cohesive strategy making down through the hierarchy becomes easier to achieve when company strategy is distilled into pithy, easy to grasp terminology that can be used to drive consistent strategic action throughout the company.

❖ The greater amount of company's strategic personnel who knows, understanding and make to the company's basic direction and looking for strategy, it is the smaller the risk that people and organization units will go off in conflict strategic directions towards crafting strategy and achieve the mission and vision of the company.

❖ Many strategic people are given a strategy making role when strategic decision making is pushed down to Frontline levels.

❖ Good communication of strategic themes and guiding principles of among themes members, thus it serves a valuable strategy unifying the company's vision and mission purpose.

❖ A company's strategic plan lays out its future direction, performance targets and strategy.

❖ Development of a strategic vision, setting objectives, and crafting a strategy is the basic direction setting tasks of a company.

❖ In this stage involves mapping out the company's direction that based on its short-term and long range performance targets and competitive moves and internal action approached, these can be used in achieving the targeted business results.

❖ Crafting strategically constitute a strategic plan for coping with industry and competitive conditions, it is the expected actions of the industry's key players, challenges and issues that stand as obstacles to the company's success.

Figure—2.2 : Structuring Strategic Decisions

Figure 2.2 exhibit the strategic structuring decisions are based inputs from a variety of assessments are relevant. Strategic decisions based on three types of assessments are outlined below:

❖ The first stage is concerned organizational strengths and weaknesses.
❖ Second stage is concerned evaluates the competitor strengths, weaknesses and strategies.
❖ A third stage is concerned assesses the competitive context in the form of the customers and their needs, the market, and the market environment.

STAGE 4: IMPLEMENTING AND EXECUTING THE STRATEGY

Managing strategy, implementation and execution of strategy is in operation oriented. It involves certain activity which aimed at shaping the performance of core business activities in a company. It is a supportive manner in a company. These things are easily and the most demanding to firms and it can be time consuming part of the strategy management and implementation process in firms. The strategic manager takes special initiative for converting strategic plans into actions and results are able to cope and direct organizational change, in this way motivates people, build and strengthen company competencies and competitive capabilities, create a strategy which works in better climate and either meet or beat standard performance targets in a company. **Strategy Implementation planning of a company determines the critical success factors and establishes change programs to implement the strategic initiatives to achieve superior goals and objectives of an organization.**

Managing strategy, implementation and execution of strategy process include the following principal aspects:

- ❖ Trained and skilled staffing in the organization that consciously building and strengthening strategy supportive competencies and competitive capabilities and organizing the work effort in this achieve strategy. Microsoft always retains talented employees at any cost.
- ❖ Development of budget that guide to company how to efficient utilization of ample resources into those activities critical to strategic success.
- ❖ It ensures that policies, objectives and operating procedures facilities rather than impede effective execution.
- ❖ A company can be using the best known practices to perform core business activities and pushing for continuous improvement.
- ❖ Installation information or software and operating systems which ensures to company personnel to better use and carry out their strategic roles day in and day out.
- ❖ Motivating is the special tool to top level management of the company, it is useful to motivate their employees and to pursue the target objectively energetically.

❖ Providing incentives and rewards to employees who have done excellent achievement performance, objectives which is the output of better strategy execution.

❖ Crafting culture of th e company and its work climate conducive to successful strategy implementation and execution.

❖ Exerting and internal leadership that's needed to drive for implementation forward and try to keep on improving strategy execution in the business. The organization has responsibility to take appropriate decisions on the basis of strengths, weakness of the firms.

Good strategy execution involves creating strong which is "fits" between strategy and organizational capabilities and executed by the skilled top level management in the enterprise, it is based between strategy and the reward structure. And also it is between strategy and internal operating systems, and between strategy and the organizational climate and culture in a company.

STAGE 5: MONITORING DEVELOPMENTS, EVALUATING AND MAKING CORRECTIVE ADJUSTMENTS

❖ Monitoring developments, evaluating and making corrective adjustments are one of the magnificent and significant stages in strategic management.

❖ A company's strategy formulation, implementation and monitoring developments, evaluating and making corrective adjustments are never final: it is a continuous process for dramatic changes in terms of improvement.

❖ An effective managing strategy is an ongoing process; it is not now and then the task of the company.

❖ It involves being evaluated the company's process, assessing the impact of new external developments and making corrective adjustments which relate to the company's vision, objectives, policies and execution of strategy into different methods in companies.

- This stage, decides whether to continue or change the company's mission and vision and objectives.
- Company's strategist always gives directions relating to strategy which seem well to be matched industry and competition and performance targets are being met in this way strategist may decide to stay the course.
- Well defined, planned and fine tuning strategic plan and continuing with ongoing efforts to improve strategy execution are sufficient in a company.
- The company can be developing appropriate strategies and its directions which are coping and overcome encounters disruptive changes in its external environment.
- Poor strategy monitoring impacts to the company's business and reduce its operation efficiency in terms of profit, sales and customer base. For avoiding the poor strategy monitoring, a company must take corrective action when evaluation of strategy and try to avoid to poor monitoring, poor execution.
- External and internal conditions of the company, a strategist reformulate a suitable strategy, to make proper objectives, mission, vision and policy and appropriate direction towards the growth and development of the company's performance in terms of competitive advantages and core competence.
- A company ready and expected to modify changes its strategic vision, direction, objectives, and strategy over time in business.
- Proficient strategy execution provides an opportunity to firms for learning about new things, changes from the internal and external environment.
- Well defined strategy execution and good assessment of company performance which is needed for improving the company's normal and desirable results.
- Strategy execution is continuously searching the dramatic changes for improvement in this way making corrective adjustments whenever and wherever a company is required.

Strategic Alternatives

Strategic alternatives are leading a magnificent role in planning perspective. Strategic alternatives always develop alternatives for strategy formulation, implementation and control of short term and long term planning perspective in companies. When every company has not achieved its mission a vision. It looks for alternative strategies for direction to manage, formulate with uncertain conditions and implement risk position in the company. Strategist aware and know impact of alternative plan with the safeguarding of stakeholders of a company. When choices are available to formulate policy, it is a tedious operation to select right strategy.

CHAPTER 3

CORPORATE OBJECTIVES

"Never had an objective to sell a low-cost phone"
that would compete on some level with the dirt—
cheap Android handsets that have been flooding
into emerging markets. Instead, Cook says that the
goal with the iPhone 5c was "to sell a great phone
and provide a great experience, and we figured out
a way to do it at a lower cost."

Apple CEO Tim Cook

INTRODUCTION

A company has defined set of corporate objectives and its team
consider particular objectives and targets for various areas in terms
of markets and customers: sales growth, market shares, product
reliability, delivery, customer satisfaction, learning and development,
innovation, technology upgrade, continuous improvement in services,
retain the talented employees, motivate to employees, provide social
responsibility to society, enhance educational skills of customers,
clients, vendors who are interested about company's products and
services. Corporate Objectives must reach across teams, helping
break down the silos that lead to conflicts or block attainment of
goals. Objectives must be simple and concrete, and must be presented
in a common language that all parties understand. Incentives and
compensation should link to achievement of those strategic goals.
Objectives can be delegated and cascaded to groups or individuals
in an organization. The company's CEO and strategic team take
responsibility for the development of short term and long term

objectives, plan and policies designed to produce profitable venture, it is the prime responsibility of a corporate strategic team. Each member understands and bounding to work with established corporate policies, procedures, instructions, and working with subordinates and attainable day to day business operation and make adapt wherever change is applied. Corporate strategic team actively associated among the employee force, and clients for further attainment of objectives. A company must establish and maintain two way communication process and welcome questions and ideas.

All successful companies like Apple, Microsoft, Samsung and Google are good objectives and strategies. These companies leaders are well defined the overall strategy of the company and then delegate high level objectives to the next layer of the organization, breaking each objective into smaller, measurable targets in each level. This allows individuals who work in a company to understand their functional roles, responsibilities, how they are being measured and how their work contributes to the overall objectives. Corporate objectives ensure that optimal resource allocation-by aligning resources with the organization's strategic objectives.

IMPORTANCE OF OBJECTIVES

Company leaders enable business plan that is the outcome of the vision and mission of a company. The vision of company always concern with LONG TERM operational objectives and mission always concerns with SHORT TERM operational objectives. A company objectives are Specific, Measurable, Narrow, Concrete Tactical-short-range, set by company leaders to accomplish goals. It is a statement of attainment, time targeted, and measurable target and achieve these objectives within a stipulated time.

Company objectives are associated with Innovative transform knowledge, knowledge develops innovative features and technology oriented products and services. Consumers like innovative technology advance products. A company leader always finds a new technology platform to produce products, selling the products and development of brand, image, value and sustainability and attractive customer. A company wishes to achieve its superior objectives.

Corporate objectives have protected employees, produce products and services environmentally friendly matter in the way protect natural resources. Powerful objectives special focus has provided training who are working with proper training and diversity, the objective cannot overrule economically perform, operating margin, free cash flow return on assets, level of investments. Consider environmental policy: for protecting end-of-life their recovery, number of sites with a certified environmental management system. A good objectives always talks about Production: manufacturing cost per tire, production capacities, flexibility and the marketing of technology products across the globe.

Corporate Strategy is an ongoing process that develops both long-term and short-term objectives at the corporate level, business level and operational levels, establishes and/or modifies the organizational hierarchy to manage operational processes, and determine the suitability, feasibility and acceptability of the strategy and achieve the superior objectives of a company.

Well define Planning is the most important functions of any company. As the old saying goes, "Failing to plan is planning to fail". Setting goals and objectives is the first and most critical step in the planning process. Company leaders always need to be sure all employees are well trained in how to set these important performance measurements.

NEED FOR LONG TERM AND SHORT TERM CORPORATE OBJECTIVES

A company long term and short term objectives are initiated, target, performance, rules supported, measures the business performance, meet shareholders expectations, and influence of clients internal or external environment of a company. Objectives enable to evaluate strengths, weakness, opportunities and threats of a company and its helpful development of business activities across the globe.

A corporate team has experience in new product development, technology transfers, meeting unexpected challenges of domestic and international business, especially in the development of business operation commercialization. A corporate strategic team bound to possess technical, commercial and financial acumen platform to form objectives of an enterprise. A company can set and formulate financial and strategic objectives. These objectives are based on the both short-term and long term performance relating to business. Short term or annual objectives focus too and attention to delivering immediate performance improvement in the current year. Long term objectives focus on the long term prosperity of firm's or companies.

LONG TERM CORPORATE OBJECTIVES

Objectives are helpful for the development of core values such as innovation, excellent customer services, and value base social responsibility towards society. Short run profit maximization is rarely based on the best approach to achieving sustained corporate growth and profitability of the firm. It is recognized by the strategic managers of the firm. Therefore, to achieve long term prosperity purpose strategic managers designed long term objectives. A corporate strategic team enables to values, empowerment, career and skill development of employees, continuous improvement and grow core business, able to keep and maintain market leadership and enhance market share, loyalty and commitment to provide services to customers, build strategic alliances, joint ventures with leading producing innovative products platform, and funds invested for employees skills development, retain talented intellectual resources, and make facilities for well supply chain system. These things will be considered at the time of development of Long term objectives of the firm or company or organization as listed below:

- Profitability
- Productivity
- Competitive position
- Employees development
- Employee relationships
- Public responsibility
- Technological leadership

Profitability

Value creation enables profitability of a company. Profitability is an important functional area of the long-term objectives of the firm. The ability of any business to operate in the long run depends on attaining an acceptable level of profits. Strategically managed firms characteristically have a profit objective usually expressed in return on equity. A corporate Leaders (Strategist) take the necessary steps for continuous improvement of profitability of a company, Strategist assess the business environment, competitive position of the business, the structure of the production process, how the budget is allocated, strategic movement, operating results and focus on cost cutting and develop innovative technology platform to produce products and services with advanced features products and services. It decides high quality products available at low cost and develop a strong brand image. Funds invest in emerging markets and will adapt innovative business development models. It enables to marketing of products and services and gain competitive advantages. Access information and use this information for the development of the platform. Minimize delivery cost, efficiency in cost control, and conduct market analysis, demand forecast, upgraded latest technology platform and achieve superiority in providing value base services to clients.

Improves profit by focusing on cost reduction, asset optimization and revenue growth. Identify non-value added costs and establish a long-term framework for cost reduction including information and process standardization, application rationalization, organization structure and working capital improvements. Also measures for revenue enhancement.

Productivity

A company aims to achieve quality management by the application of innovative tools to measure productivity performance at competitive market. A strategic team ensures to technology upgrading platform and reach to target customers when products are innovative, quality, advance features, low cost, cost advantage. Top management and middle level functional managers are ready to apply all market segments and special care for research and development department. Technology driving change also leads to Productivity and it is an essential need for each strategist in the corporation. Strategic managers try to improve the productivity of their systems. Companies that can improve the input-output relationship normally increase profitability. Productivity objectives are sometimes stated in terms of desired decreases in most. This is an equally effective way to increase profitability. **Constant product innovation** (at least two upgrades and one new product launch) to prolong the product Lifecycle which will help in maintaining and growing the market share

Competitive Position

We have to compare Smartphone to Smartphone mobile companies like Samsung, Apple, Microsoft. These companies mainly talking about the features of the Smartphone and its price and facilities available to customers. **Apple is looking for emerging markets to introduce new Smartphone.** Apple's latest Smartphones are the iPhone 5S and iPhone 5C. **China and India are** the world's largest

Smartphone market. Apple's compete among the player in Smartphone market with Motorola, Samsung, Microsoft, and new rivals such as Xiaomi of China and Micromax of India. Apple upgrades its products and renovated its top of the line Smartphone with the 5S, expanded the iPhone line with the 5C, and released iOS 7, the most significant upgrade to its mobile operating system in years.

A company finds it's Competitive Positioning, Where to compete in terms of Markets, Products, Channels Network and a company should know How to compete with Industry Value Chain, Financial structure effective cash flow strategy and maximize utilization of Internal Capabilities, belief and trust which held by the people of company about the company, core process network, fundamental resources network platform as People, capital, technology and effective and efficient organizational structure.

Competitive position can increase profitability and productivity of the company. Companies or firms or organization's, Competitive position reduces the cost of production of the output. The corporate success depends on the firm's competitive position. It is strongly dominated in the market. It influences few things such as customer related objectives like launch new innovative products to keep the loyal customers intact, build new customer base and gain competitive advantage over the competitors.

Develop a strategic approach to grow market share in emerging markets like China, Africa and India. In India Apple iPhone is still ranked after android supported phones. Smartphone market Apple has a strong competitive position comparing to Google, Microsoft and some other companies in the world. Apple is bringing the best quality Smartphone at low cost and introduce across the world. It gains competitive position. Location is the plus point of gaining competitive position for software giant Microsoft, IBM, TCS, Infosys etc.

Employee Development

It refers to experienced and core skills employees are the asset of the organization. For long-term purposes, the company's employees need training for further course of action that effectively and efficiently managed to produce productivity in the competitive position. Therefore, it is one of the major long-term objectives of the organization. A company invest funds for employee development in terms of how to interactions with customers, train the employees about study the consumers behavior and psychology for buying of products and its accessories, it specify customer support in the form of repairs and accessories availabity to customers, and company able to conduct training programmes for how to sell technology features products, to measure and identify who are the target customers, updated training the skills like conceptual skills, human skills, and effective manage customers and offering to innovative ideas and build trust about quality about products, services, after sales services facilities and explain the genuine reasons to buy company products and similar products pros and cons and finally customers are trust the company and its products. First and foremost, employees got to understand the business. Two, company leader look for employees who are aggressive in wanting to create new things and do different things and collaborate. Company leader needs people with emotional and intellectual stamina. Being a business leader in this world today is 24/7. Do employees aspire to that? Do they have a sense of courage about their point of view? Are they persistent? Those are attitudinal things that we see early on.

Employee Relationships

All companies actively seek good employee who committed relations with organizational environment. **Each member of a company is expected and required to take responsibilities, to work and promote in the interest of an organization and conduct its business within the framework of corporate policies and make**

facilities to work with clients. The strategic manager should know the employee needs and expectations. Strategic managers take a decision to welfare program for the employees of the companies. It can be improved the employee's relationship within an organization. Business leader always supports the employee to be learning & growth and achieve the superior objectives of a company. **A company empower employees work and commitment to work in the workplace. Any company provides core respect for individuals, and expect the best customer services, and the superior accomplishment of all tasks.** Company leaders are trying to Reduce employee rate of attrition at middle to top management level.

Talent retention is a most important job in the fast moving technology industry where every day there is a new company being formed and sold for billions USD. The success for any company lies within the skill of human resource it has. Thus, it's very important to retain the talents at middle to top level management which is involved in strategic decision making and confidential product research.

The customer support team always supports and train customer representative with company and clients. It deals with employees' problems, prospectus and take care for learning new skills, able cope with top level, middle level and effectively and efficiently to discharge duties irrespective partiality. A company main aim is to develop superior and employee relationships within the company employees and outside clients. A strategic team will motivate their employees to do their performance in the superior manner. Employees are frequently met with their clients and dare to ask questions and answer and plan for the future by keeping an open mind to new ideas.

Technological Leadership

A company develops high-tech product and services. Managing peak technological performance is a very difficult task of strategic team is working in an organization. Without funding, resources but companies such as Microsoft, IBM, Apple, Google and others have technology but it is marketable and get the funds and scarce resources to manage other things in a workplace. Technological leadership can give a clear picture of the organization goals and objectives for the long term changes in the business scenario many companies state their objectives in terms of their technological leadership. Develop Research and Development department to identify future product innovation and development opportunities. Well technological leadership defines task, roles, advance commitment to work, new products, and sure to solutions for enterprise problems. Leader foster innovation through long term investment in the field research and development, accelerate production by using technology and retain talented, skilled, knowledgeable intellectual resources in an organization. Leaders will be sharing the knowledge, learning process, skills and develop an international platform for accelerating company products, performance, values, sustainable development. The leader brings faster, smaller, more cost-efficient and power-efficient technological solutions to the marketplace.

Public Responsibility

A Corporate's engagement is the prime responsibility, it is the philosophy of a company bringing about global social change, key initiatives and priorities, how they measure success, collaborating across sectors, challenges to progress and much more. Business recognizes their social responsibilities towards to customer and society. Public responsibility is build up long-term images in the society by through providing social work in public. A company's management board and its employees are engaging social service activities and engaged nonprofit services to the general public. A company respects competitors, and respect of law. A company must believe long term public interest is the best way to serve by platform competing other enterprises. A company encourage to their employees to ready to take public responsibility for superior performance in all areas of work.

QUALITIES OF LONG TERM OBJECTIVES

A company develops qualities that are superior accomplished all qualities. Any business enterprise produces quality products and services of the most advanced design platform, and fix at the lowest possible cost. Strategic team aware the advances made by other companies, and make better them where we can and willing to adapt them whenever fit their needs. A strategist quality work will make quality company. A company is working with the aim of the outstanding output of products and services, customer services and human relations. When a company quality is lost, it results that lost the brand name and reputation. When an enterprise offers quality products and services to clients, it recognized it. Today, competitors also offering quality products and services to client but a good and advanced quality products and services delivering to clients with the highest level of quality and ready to improve quality such company become a future leader in a business. A company establishes quietly in work defect free quality in a work. Each work do defect free quality work, it will pass next process, the end product will be defect free product. It shows that quality leadership in performance of job with the defect free work.

Any superior performance all levels of a company give importance and commitment to quality of products, services, solutions to clients. Quality is the fundamental component of the value of a company. A company focusses for improvement of quality services and committed to upgrade in quality products, solutions and services.

Acceptable

Quality acceptable when any companies achieve consistency, efficiency and predictability with software quality that meets objectives while success or failure often times depends on whose products or services are the highest quality. It results that provide unique capabilities to help organizations ensure the functionality, usability, reliability and performance of delivering products and services exceed their customers' expectations. Cut the risk and cost of product and service delivery while improving products and service quality.

Acceptable measures in companies are likely accepted by the strategic managers to pursue the objectives. Quality objectives are consistent with perceptions and the preference of the company mission and vision. Even if certain long term objectives are frequently designed to be acceptable to major interest groups external to the company.

Flexible

Today's work environment is flexible and its connections, collaborations, and user choice, that enables the enables the worker to be more agile and perform activities anywhere, anytime-and can ultimately help create greater enterprise value. Today's workers increasingly meet, share, discover and get work done via technology. They expect the technology tools they have embraced in their personal lives to play an important part in their business lives, as well. This poses important challenges for the organization supporting the workplace.

Long-term objectives should be modifiable in the event of the extraordinary changes due to environmental forecasts. At the same time, flexibility is usually increased at the expenses of specific events of the firms. Likewise, employee confidence may be tempered; therefore, an adjustment of a flexible objective may affect their job. Today's workers increasingly meet, share, discover and get work done via technology. They expect the technology tools they have embraced in their personal lives to play an important part in their business lives, as well. This poses important challenges for the organization supporting the workplace. Mobility makes the flexible workplace work, and it is the attribute most in demand by end users. The tools that support users-applications and information-need to go where business is taking place.

Forward thinkers are keenly focused on improving enterprise performance through collaboration. They are leveraging social business to strengthen two-way communication and sharing-both within the organization and with customers, vendors and partners. Forward thinkers are making fast use of emerging mobile devices, operating systems, platforms and applications. They recognize that the bring-your-own-device trend is expanding and, rather than trying to limit usage, they are supporting a broader set of devices and operating systems. They are investing in a mobile application platform and creating application stores that favor collaborative and content applications for core business processes versus the back office.

Measurable

Companies Objectives must clearly and precisely measure in business. It clearly states what will be achieved and with what time frame. Objectives should measure because of misunderstanding of long-term objectives of the company. Performance, productivity, efficiency, security, data analytics, processing and management, storage capacity, collaboration and connectivity concerns impact virtually every organization-large and small. If capabilities and processes aren't evolved to keep pace with new challenges and demands, economic and competitive pressures mount.

Motivating

Research studies indicate the people are most productive when objectives are set at a motivating level. This is the major problem for individuals and groups. Therefore, they are different in their perceptions of high enough. One valuable recommendation to strategic managers is to develop multiple objectives to motivating to individual and specific groups in the company. Motivated the workers to do more than their very best. Since jobs are no longer guaranteed because the company is losing money, the complacent mindset, it is disturbed and employees are motivated to work harder, do better than their best, and most importantly, produce results for the company. A team that can inspire employees to work harder by giving them a goal and helping them reach that goal. Managers informed their employees of the broad goal to show them where their work fit as a strategy to motivate them to reach the goal. We know example of IBM how IBM is motivating its employees:

"A major HR challenge is how to motivate and retain more than 300,000 employees around the world to be smart, innovative and committed to winning in a fiercely competitive environment. That's why IBM values education and encourages and enables its employees to grow, learn and develop both professionally and personally. As a result, the HR team offers more than 40,000 classrooms and e-learning Internet courses for professional development to employees around the global, and many opportunities for personal growth in the civic, trade, professional and non-profit sectors. **IBM motivates its employees through:**

- ❖ Performance-based opportunities.
- ❖ Leadership.
- ❖ Hiring diverse and talented people.
- ❖ Flexibility.
- ❖ A values-based climate.

But what role does HR play in building the ideal IBM workforce?. Again, at IBM, the goals are clear.

Suitable

Long-term objectives are suitable to the broad aims of the organization or company. It clearly expressed in the statement of the company mission and vision. Each objective should be a step toward attainment of the overall goals.

Understandable

Strategic managers clearly understand at all levels in the organization for the accomplishment of objectives. Corporate leaders should understand major criteria for monitoring and evaluating of the organizational mission and vision.

Achievable

It is the last long term quality objectives of the organization. Achievable strategies always focus on the mission and vision of the organization or company. It is a very difficult task to strategist to face complex external difficulties in the business. Strategist designs a suitable strategy for implementation for the achievement of the goals and objectives of the company or firms or organization.

- ❖ In total, objectives should be quantitative, measurable, realistic, understandable, challenging, hierarchical, obtainable and concurrent among organizational units in the business.
- ❖ Each objective can be associated with a timeline of the company. Objectives generally stated in terms of growth of assets, sales volume, market share, diversification of business activities, earning per share and social responsibility towards the stakeholders of the company.
- ❖ Clearly defined objectives are definitely brought excellent benefits to the company.
- ❖ Objectives can be provided valuable and suitable direction, allow synergy, aid evaluation, establishes priorities, reduce uncertainty, minimize conflicts, stimulate exertion and aid in both the allocation of resources and the design of jobs in a company.
- ❖ Short range objectives can be identical to long range objectives if an organization is already performing at the targeted long range level.
- ❖ Short range objectives are related to the current year business trends, development of business policy within a year. Long

term objectives will not be affecting the short term goals and objectives of the firm's.

CONCEPT OF STRATEGIC INTENT

❖ When a company pursues ambitious strategic objectives and concentrates its full resources and competitive actions on achieving that objectives i.e. strategic intent exhibit in the company.

❖ Company objectives sometimes play another role like signaling unmistakable strategic intent to make quantum gains in competing against key rivals and establish itself as a clear cut winner in the marketplace and enhance core competency and resources in the company.

❖ It can be dominant in company within the industry in terms of unseating the existing industry leader, delivering the best customer service of any company and turning a new technology into products and services which capable of changing the way people work and live in the company.

❖ Ambitious companies strategic intent to be invariable due to proportion to their immediate capabilities and market positions.

THE NEED FOR OBJECTIVES AT ALL ORGANIZATIONAL LEVELS

Business leaders today are facing many challenges and opportunities in today's growingly complex. A corporate need objectives at all organization levels of constant improvement of its products', platform, technical performance and its tire-related services' quality. It develops innovative platform such as new technologies, product to support sustainable mobility. Managing of the right customer.

❖ The objectives are to be formulated by the top level management in all organizations.

❖ Setting of objectives needs to be broken down into performance targets for each separate business, product line, functional department and individual work unit in the company.

❖ Company performance can't reach full potential without clearly defined objectives in each area of the organization. It contributes directly to the desired company wide customs and results.

❖ Strategic and financial objectives are set to performance targets for each organizational unit which support rather than conflict with or without negotiable the achievement of company.

CHAPTER 4

GENERIC STRATEGIES FOR COMPANIES

INTRODUCTION

Business leader understands and achieve best in class operational efficiency, quality & functional excellence, innovation and progressive improvement in quality products and services. The business CEO knows the profit, success and progressive growth, all these accomplished through an intelligent, articulate and well-crafted business strategy. Company success or failure depends on strategy and its brand name: it establishes customer loyalty towards companies products and services.

A company business operation either success or failure depends on markets, competition, industry changes, adapting business models, and mergers, acquisitions and divestitures etc.,. A business leader become a master of these areas, otherwise, willing to learn and strive to master in order to drive ongoing business success. Generic strategies are closely associated with the five forces of any company business. The five forces are buyer power, supplier power, threat of substitute products and services, threat of new entrants and rivalry among existing competitors.

Toyota achieves its cost leadership strategy by adopting lean production, careful choice and control of suppliers, efficient distribution, and low servicing costs of a quality product.

GENERIC STRATEGIES

A company generic strategy expert can define and understand market drivers, innovative value propositions, risks, technology strategies, globalization, Merger and Acquisition activity and the development of new business models. The Generic strategy implements in an enterprise, an expert can understand and leverage core competencies to drive real value by formulating leading-edge, implementable strategies that result in sustainable growth and profitability.

Michael Porter's Generic Strategies helpful to corporate leaders. Corporate leaders today are addressing many challenges and opportunities in today's growing and changing business operation, update changes, innovation, enhance market to clients etc., introduction of technological capabilities to drive innovation in business models, and across customers, markets and channels in order to create growth and sustainable advantage.

Generic strategies developed by Michael Porter's and applied in business operation. According to Michael Porter's, a choosing business strategy in a company, it must gains competitive advantage to a company. Strategic Group of a company may be chosen from three generic competitive approaches to achieve long term objectives of a company. They are as listed below:

- ❖ Cost leadership/low cost
- ❖ Differentiation
- ❖ Focus

These strategies are known as generic strategies, and these strategies are applicable to all business or industries. A company can pursue them regardless of whether they are manufacturing, service or not-for-profit organizations. Generic strategies results to a company will be making consistent choices on product, market and distinctive competencies to achieve superior objectives.

The product/market distinctive-competing choices and generic competitive strategies at business level industries are listed below:

- ❖ Cost leadership
- ❖ Differentiation
- ❖ Focus

And its choices as listed below:

- ❖ Product differentiation
- ❖ Market segmentation
- ❖ Distinctive competency

Michael Porter's calls these strategies as generic strategies. Cost leadership strategy emphasizes to be producing standardized products at a very low per unit cost for consumers who are price sensitive. Differentiation strategy aims to be producing products and services which are considered unique in industry wide and directed towards to consumers who are relatively price insensitive.

- ❖ Michael Porter's imply different organizational arrangements and make careful and proper control procedures and designed to be appropriate incentive systems for human resources in the enterprise.
- ❖ In the case of the larger firms with greater accessibility of resources which typically compete on a cost leadership or differentiation basis.
- ❖ In the case of smaller firms often compete on a focus basis in business.

Microsoft, Samsung, Apple, Google, IBM, are well in competitive advantage in terms of technology, innovation, change, value sustainable, brand image, corporate culture, and innovative platform to introduce new products and services to existing, old, and new clients. Porter gives stresses to need for strategists to perform cost benefit analyses to evaluate the sharing opportunities which are existed among the company's and potential strategic business units. When sharing activities and resources that enhances competitive advantage by lowering costs or raising differentiation in company's. In additionally, prompting sharing, Porter stresses the need for company's to transfer skills and expertise among existing autonomous business units effectively in order to gain competitive advantage. These are depending upon the type of industry, size of the firm and the nature of competition, various strategies could yield major advantages in the form of cost leadership, differentiation, and focus.

COST LEADERSHIP STRATEGIES

Apple gain cost leadership strategies to introduce new version of Smartphone in emerging market India, China, and world market. Simultaneously, Samsung competes with the Smartphone market by taking advantage cost leadership strategies. A company sell products at low cost compare to competitor in the domestic and international market. It is possible only when would take competitive advantage in terms of company efficiency, size, scale, scope and cumulative experience. A company's goal in pursuing a cost leadership or low cost strategy is to out perform competitors by doing everything. It can to pursue goods or service at a cost lower than their competitors. Cost leadership strategy is required strategies choice of product and service into different market segments and its competitors. It will be pursued in conjunction with differentiation. Cost leadership strategies are gaining to forward, backward and horizontal integration strategies. A successful cost leadership strategy usually utilization of the entire company's strength and opportunities in the form of higher efficiency, low overhead, limited perks to human resources, minimize the waste, intensive screening of the budget and its tools like income and expenditure, effective using the wide span control, rewards linked to cost containment, and broad employee participation in cost control efforts in the firm's in this reduce the cost of the product and services.

Any company achieve cost leadership strategy. It will possibly when a company takes transformation strategy supports for continuing desire to remain the marketplace leader and fulfilled needs to drive productivity, cost reduction, and ensures supply security, continuity and quality for customers. This strategy will be executed while sustaining industry leadership in supplier diversity, environmental affairs and social responsibility. A company is willing to produce goods and services at low cost with high quality and technological progressiveness. Tata's management focused on reducing costs, improving efficiencies and managing cash flow. Restructure its workforce, cutting jobs, it is one way to reduce cost of production. Cost leadership strategy of IBM. It is aiming to deliver cost reduction, both internally and externally for clients. Any company will take cost leadership advantage it bound to demonstrate that significant cost reduction and management will take bold action and determined engagement at executive level. A strategy group helps to manage people who are ready to take a decision related to the key issues quickly, setting the direction for deploying cross-functional capabilities including process improvement, IT efficiency, business model change and outsourcing. A company bound to achieve cost leadership strategies when it does certain things are staff reduction, workload alteration, technology utilization, and process engineering. Accenture takes a holistic and intelligent approach to total cost reduction, either for operating advantage to produce rapid economic value, or for structural advantage, with a focus on sustained efficiency and long-term growth.

A company strategist does these things restructure a company, create value and enhance brand image, don't cut cost research and development brings new technology update feature products. Eliminates waste, improve operational efficiency and performance, retain intellectual and focus on marketing and create a brand image and able to manage people cost. Management reduces costs and risks, increases revenue and optimizes asset utilization while prices are lower than competitors', prices economy of scale, corporate culture, competitive advantage and optimum utilization of scarce resources.

Advantages of Cost leadership Strategy

A company ready to take competitive advantage to implement cost leadership strategy at business level, industry level and corporation level.

There are two advantages occurring from cost leadership strategy. They are as mentioned below:

❖ Cost leadership strategy refers to lower costs of product and service offered by the company, the cost leader is able to charge a lower price than its competitors. The cost leader makes a higher profit than its competitors because of its lowers costs of products and service. A company achieves it through economy of scale of producing quality products and services. Best example is the Apple introduces new version of Smartphone and take competitive advantage with Samsung, Microsoft, and Google. Google has a competitive advantage over Microsoft and others in competing online search and advertising business.

❖ When industry rivalry increases and a company start to compete on low price at highly advanced technology featured quality products and services. The cost leader will be able to withstand competition start to compete on price; the cost leader will be able to withstand completion better than other companies because of its lower costs. For both reasons, cost leaders are likely to earn above-average profits.

Disadvantages of Cost Leadership Strategy

Important disadvantages of cost leadership strategy are outlined:

❖ The principal dangers of the cost-leadership approach risk in competitors ability to find ways of producing at lower cost and beat the cost leader.

❖ When a company under perform its performance and it is an adverse effect on the company cost leadership strategy. For instance, Nokia is unable take competitive advantage in the Smartphone market, it's loose market, and finally merged with Microsoft. Microsoft ready to take competitive advantage of Nokia values, services, brand image, these facilities used by Microsoft and introduce in new Windows phone to emerging markets.

❖ Competitor's ability to easily imitate the cost leader's method is another threat to the cost leadership strategy.

❖ The cost leadership strategy carries a risk that the cost leader, the single-minded desire to reduce costs, may lose right to changes in customer tastes.

Strategic Choices

The company cost leader strategy is choosing a low level of product differentiation. Differentiation is expensive for the company; if the company expands resources to make its product unique than its costs rise. The cost leader aims for a level of differentiation not marketing inferior to that of the differentiator (a company competes by spending resources on product development) but a level obtainable at low cost.

The cost leader also normally ignores the different market segments and positions. Its product is to appeal to the average customer. The main reason is that the cost leader makes it choice by developing a line of products and tailored to the needs of different market segments. It is an expensive proposition. A cost leader normally engages to only a limited amount of market segmentation. Customer happy when the company normally charges a lower price than its competitors attracts customers to its products and service.

In developing distinctive competencies, the overriding goal of the cost leader must be to develop competencies. It enables to increase its efficiency and lower its costs compared with its competitors. The development of distinctive competencies in manufacturing and material management is central to achieving this goal. Companies are pursuing a low cost strategy may attempt to ride down the experience therefore; they can lower their manufacturing costs. Achieving a low cost position may also require that the company develop skills in flexible manufacturing and adopt develop skills in flexible manufacturing and adapt efficient materials-management techniques.

DIFFERENTIATION STRATEGY

Apple differentiates its products iPods, iPads, and iPhones from its competition. Apple has a strong differentiation strategy built strong fans across the world over competitor Samsung.

Differentiation is a strategy, it practice by a company to gain a competitive advantage over its competitors. A company will make a differentiation in terms of product, services, personnel, channel and image differentiation. It strategy refers to the differentiated company's ability to satisfy a customer need. A differentiation strategy should be pursued only after a careful study of buyer's needs and prefer to determine the feasibility of incorporating one or more unique product features. It helps company to charge a premium price; a price considerably above the industry average. The company's ability to increase by charging premium prices (rather than by reducing costs of the output) allows the differentiator to outperform its competitors and gain above average profits. The premium price is usually substantially above the price charged by the cost leader, and customers pay it therefore, they believe the product-differentiated qualities to be worth the difference. Successful differentiation provides greater product flexibility, greater compatibility, lower costs, improved services, less maintenance, greater convenience or more features in this strategy.

Apple makes the product different consistently products offering to customers. Its unique features include its design, functionality, durability, and consistency of all products and services. Its products are sleek and simplistic.

Samsung is providing a cheaper and lesser iPhone, it's differentiated itself with larger screens, different features, successful marketing, and delivering what consumers want.

Products can be differentiated in a number of ways a company will stand apart from standardized products:

- ❖ Superior quality
- ❖ Unusual or unique features
- ❖ More responsive customer service
- ❖ Rapid product innovation
- ❖ Advanced technological features
- ❖ Engineering design
- ❖ Additional features
- ❖ An image of prestige or status

One strategy to win the competition is differentiation strategy. Differentiation strategy highlights the striking difference in its brand with competitive brands. Product differentiation may come from a variety of factors, including product quality, product features, durability, reliability, exceptional product design, reliability, easy to fix and styles. Consisting of product quality and quality of performance quality conformity. Quality refers to the level of performance where it operates the product characteristics. Is the product low performance levels, on average, high or super. IBM, using a product differentiation strategy based on the quality of performance.

Toyota's use both differentiation and low cost as generic strategies to try and gain a competitive advantage over their competitors in the automotive industry. Toyota differentiates on several levels from their competitors. First of all, Toyota has been very successful in differentiating on the basis of superior design and quality. This has led to Toyota being able to create a brand image that is very strong and one that brings to mind quality, long lasting cars when a potential customer sees it.

Advantages of Differentiation Strategy

Advantages of differentiation strategy as outlined :

- ❖ The company's unit price must be higher than that of the average company and its unit cost must be equivalent to that of the average company.
- ❖ The company's unit must be lower than that of the average company and
- ❖ Its unit price must be equivalent to that of the average company
- ❖ The company must have both a lower unit and a higher unit price than the average company.

Disadvantages of Differentiation Strategy

Major disadvantages of differentiation strategy are listed below:

- ❖ Developing the distinctive competency needed to provide a differentiation advantage is often expensive to company.
- ❖ A differential cost usually has higher costs than the cost leader.
- ❖ The main problems with the differentiation strategy center on the company's long-term ability to maintain its perceived uniqueness in customers' eye on the market.
- ❖ A differentiation strategy is the ease to competitors can imitate a differentiator product and the difficulty of maintaining a premium price.

Strategic Choice of Differentiation strategy

Lenovo, Samsung, Apple, Microsoft, Micromax, Carbon, Nokia and Sony companies' differentiation strategy different from design, functionality and features. The differentiate strategy chooses a high level of product differentiation to gain a competitive advantage.

Differentiation can be achieved with quality, innovation and responsive a product appeal to customers' psychological desires can become a source of differentiation. A company pursues a differentiation strategy strives to differentiate itself along as many dimensions as possible. The less it resembles its rival, the more it is protected from competition, and the wider is its market appeal.

A differentiator chooses to market segment. The company offers a product to design for each market differentiator, but a company chooses to serve just niches where it has a specific differentiation advantage.

A differentiated company concentrates on the organizational function that provides the source of its differentiation advantage. Differentiation based on the innovation and technological competency depends on R&D function. A differentiator does not want to increase costs unnecessarily.

FOCUS STRATEGY

Toyota to focus on emerging markets. "Quality is their selling point. It's more important to overcome this quality issue than to bring out new products. Mr. Toyoda, the grandson of Toyota's founder, said growth will build on two pillars: emerging markets and eco-friendly cars". Focus strategy is the third generic competitive strategy and one of the foundations of business level strategy. Focus strategy is directed towards serving the need of a limited customer group or segment. A focus strategy is the focused company concentrates on serving a particular market niche that may be defined geographically, by type of customer, or by segment of the product line. A successful focus strategy depends on an industry segments like customer, product line, geographical segment.

Once a company has chosen its market segment, a company may pursue a focus strategy through either a differentiation or a low cost approach. A focused company is a specialized differentiator or cost leader. Because of their small size, few focus firms are able to pursue cost leadership and differentiation simultaneously. If a firm uses a low cost approach, it competes against the cost leader in the market segment where it has no cost advantage with focus strategy, a company concentrates on small volume custom products, where it has a cost and leaves the large volume standardized market to the cost leader.

Apple focus strategy latest product lines and revenue models as outlined

- ❖ A design firm
- ❖ A media platform
- ❖ A publishing company
- ❖ A software powerhouse
- ❖ A computer builder
- ❖ A movement

If a focuser pursues a differentiation approach, then all the means of differentiation that are open to the differentiators are available to the focused company. The point is that the focused company competes with the differentiator in only one or in just a few segments. Focused companies are likely to develop differentiated product qualities successfully because of their knowledge of a small customer set or knowledge of a region. Furthermore, concentrating on a small range of products. Sometimes allows a focused to develop innovations faster than a large differentiation. A focused company concentrates on building market share in one market segment and, if successful, may begin to serve more and more market segments. Microsoft's recent focus strategy on "services and devices"—essentially to become a hybrid of Microsoft's biggest competitors, Google and Apple.

Microsoft reshuffles its business in an attempt to promote faster innovation and a sharper focus software to devices and services. The move by the world's largest software maker comes amid a steady decline in demand for PCs as people turn to tablets and other mobile gadgets. How well the reorganization will help Microsoft compete with more nimble rivals like Apple and Google.

"Although we will deliver multiple devices and services to execute and monetise the strategy, the single core strategy will drive us to set shared goals for everything we do. We will see our product line holistically, not as a set of islands,"

By
CEO Steve Ballmer

Advantages of Focus Strategy

An important advantage of focus strategy as listed below:

- ❖ Focus strategy is protected from competitors to the extent therefore; it can provide a product or service.
- ❖ Focus strategy gives the focuser power over its buyer therefore; they cannot get the something from anyone also.
- ❖ It permits a company stay close to its customers and to respond to their changing needs.
- ❖ It can be developed superior skills in customer responsiveness, its based unit's ability to serve the needs of regional customer.
- ❖ These are advantages are focused on efficiency, quality, innovation and customer responsiveness of the company.

Disadvantages of Focus strategy

An important and major disadvantage of focus strategy is listed below:

- ❖ Key focuser failure due to powerful suppliers of goods and service. Therefore, the competitor is strong control of market segmentation.

❖ A large differentiator sometimes is not experience to focus strategy due to the difficulty of managing a large number of market segments.

❖ A focuser produces at a small volume, its production costs often exceed. Higher cost can also reduce profitability and even loss of the business. So that this factor has one of important disadvantages of focus strategy.

❖ The focuser's in the niche can suddenly disappear because of technological changes in customer tastes.

❖ Focuser is not concentrated of efficiency, quality, innovation and customer responsiveness, Its impact is to failure of focus strategy in a company.

Strategic Choices of Focus Strategy

The specific product/ market/ distinctive competency choice is made by a focused company. Differentiation can be high or low because the company can pursue a low-cost or differentiation approach. As for customer groups, a focused company chooses specific niches in which to compete, rather than going for the whole market, like the cost leader. A focuser may pursue any distinctive competency because it can pursue any kind of differentiation or low cost advantage.

A focused strategy company can take to develop a competitive advantage explain why they're so many small companies in relation to large ones. A focused company has enormous opportunity to develop its own niche and compete against low cost and differentiated enterprises, which tend to be larger. A focus strategy provides an opportunity for an entrepreneur to find and then exploit a gap in the market by developing an innovative product that customers cannot do without.

GENERIC STRATEGIES COMPARATIVE SKILLS AND RESOURCE REQUIREMENT

Generic strategies comparative skills and resource requirement are presented below:

Generic Strategy	Commonly Required skills and Resources	Common organizational Requirement
Overall Cost Leadership	Sustained capital investment and easily to access capital. Business process engineering skills. Intensive supervisions of labor in firm's. The low cost distribution system is existed in firms.	Tight cost control in the firms. It required frequent and detailed control reports. It structured organization responsibilities. Incentives based on meeting strict quantitative targets.
Differentiation	Strong marketing abilities in firms Product engineering in business Creative flair in firm's Strong capability in basic research in firm's Corporate reputation for quality or technological leadership Low tradition in the industry or unique combinations of skills drawn from other business Strong cooperation from channels in business	Strong coordination among function like in R&D, product development, and marketing Subjective measurement and incentives instead of quantitative measures. Amenities to attract highly skilled labor, scientists or creative people in business.

Focus	It is the combination of the above policies directed towards particular strategic target	It is the combination of the above policies directed towards the particular strategic targets

BEST COST PROVIDER STRATEGY

Samsung, Apple, Google, Microsoft and other fortune 500 companies adopted best cost provider strategy to fulfill the needs and requirement of clients from internal and external business enterprises.

Best cost provider strategy is the new model. It is the further development of three generic strategies. The five competitive generic strategies are coming under the best cost provider strategy model. This model is being pursued competitive advantage in business.

Figure—4.1 : The Five Competitive Generic Strategies

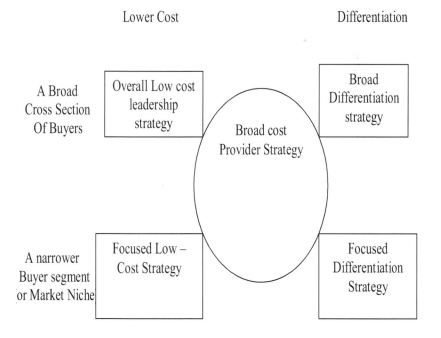

Figure 4.1 Indicates the five generic competitive strategies are outlined:

- ❖ Overall Low cost leadership strategy
- ❖ Broad Differentiation strategy
- ❖ Focused Low-Cost Strategy
- ❖ Broad cost Provider Strategy
- ❖ Focused Differentiation Strategy

DISTINCTIVE FEATURES OF THE GENERIC COMPETITIVE STRATEGIES

Distinctive features of the generic competitive strategies are presented in table:

Type of feature	Low cost Provider	Board Differentiation	Best cost provider	Focused low cost and focused Differentiation
Strategic Targets	A broad section of the market	A broad section of the market	Value conscious buyer	A narrow market niche where buyer needs and preferences are distinctively different from the rest of the market
Basic of Competitive advantage	Lower costs than competitors	An ability to offer buyers something different from competitors	More value for the money	Lower cost in serving the niche (focused low cost) or special attributes that appeal to the tastes or requirements of niche members (focused differentiation)

Market Emphasis	Try to make a virtue out of product features that lead to low cost	Build in whatever features buyers are willing to pay for Charging a premium price to cover the extra costs of differentiating features	Either underprice rival brands with comparable features or match the price of rivals and provide better features to build a reputation for delivering the best value	Communicate how the focuser's product attributes and capabilities aim at catering to niche member tastes and or specialized requirements
Sustaining the strategy	Offer economical prices/ good value Aim at contributing to a sustainable cost advantage the key is to manage costs down, year after, in every area of the business.	Communicate the points of difference incredible ways Stress constant improvement and use innovation to stay ahead of initiative competitors Concentrate on a few differentiating features; tout them to create a reputation and brand image.	Develop unique expertise in simultaneously managing costs down and upscaling features and attributes	Remain totally dedicated to serving the niche better than other competitors ; don't blunt the firm's image and efforts by entering other segments or adding other product categories to widen market appeal.
Product line	A good basic product with few frills (acceptable quality and limited selection)	Many product variations, wide, selection, strong emphasis on differentiating features	Good to excellent attributes, several to many upscale features	Features and attributes that appeal to the tastes and or special needs of the target segment.

Product emphasis	A continuous search for cost reduction without sacrificing acceptable quality and essential features	Creation of value of buyer ; strives for product superiority	Incorporation of upscale features and attributes at low cost	Tailor made for the tastes and requirements of niche members.

CHAPTER 5

GRAND STRATEGIES FOR COMPANIES

"We are rallying behind a single strategy as one company-not a collection of divisional strategies,"

By
Ballmer

INTRODUCTION

Traditional strategic planning is insufficient for addressing today's Grand strategies structures in a company turbulent time where markets move quickly and competition is increasingly vague. Grand strategies are shaping the business enterprise and focused on long term goals and objectives of a company. It is an entire business strategy of a company from starting from business to liquidation of a company. A grand strategy of Microsoft: its plan for the future emphasizes cross-product, cross-platform development across the entire Microsoft ecosystem. At a high level, Microsoft will be divided into the groups such as Marketing, Business Development and Evangelism, Advanced Strategy and Research, Finance, HR, Legal, and COO (including field support, commercial operations, and IT). Most of these areas are designed to support the engineering team, which itself is split into four groups: OS, Apps, Cloud, and Devices. The goal of this new structure is to create better synergy across products. Instead of having a different team responsible for implementing. SkyDrive support within each application area, there will be one team building a cloud application that scales across all of Microsoft's software. Microsoft's grand strategy requires key elements, some of which are already in place. It already has the Xbox, Windows Phone, and Windows deployed. Its connective tissue, SkyDrive and Bing, are still effectively incubating. Apple has the lion's share of mobile devices and media. Google dominates the search space and cloud applications. Both ate Microsoft's lunch in the Smartphone space. Most troubling, PC sales have slowed down.

Microsoft have new groups leading more products

Operating Systems Engineering Group: includes, Windows, Windows Phone, and Xbox OS. Cloud services for PCs will be in this group.

Devices and Studios Engineering Group: includes, It's the hardware group. It also has games, music, video, and entertainment.

Applications and Services Engineering Group: includes, applications in "productivity, communication, search, and other information categories." (Sounds like Office group is here.)

Cloud and Enterprise Engineering Group: includes, servers and tools, is basically keeping his gig running enterprise database and cloud stuff.

GRAND STRATEGIES/DIRECTIONAL TRATEGIES

A company's uses various strategic alternatives for achieving its growth, survival objectives. Grand strategies are also called as a master or business strategies that are intended to provide basic direction for strategic actions. The grand strategies aim is the long term sustainable development and growth of the organization.

Apple became the biggest technology company in the world by tweaking existing technologies to build magical new products. It invented its own markets—particularly with the iPod/iTunes store, with the iPhone, and with the iPad. Apple didn't build the first mp3 player, or the first smart phone, or the first tablet. But what it built became the industry leader, the standard that all other companies had to speed up to meet—in digital music, Smartphones, and tablets. Its grand strategy is to expansion of the business operation and its own a Store Just for Apple products and services, complete solutions for own products, introducing varied products, media fodder, selling products to education, highly satisfied delivery of products, outsourcing unpleasantness, and maintain consistency.

Grand strategies indicate how long range objective will be achieved. Thus, grand strategy can be defined as a comprehensive general approach that guides major actions.

Toyota's current grand strategies are product development and offensive/strategies for industry leaders. Product development is very important for Toyota due to the fact that they must come out with new fresh ideas every year in the automotive industry. If you don't develop a new design on your products, you will be left behind very quickly. Also, Toyota is an industry leader and has a lot of power because of this. Toyota stays on the offensive to keep its market share and defends against others in the industry from taking their market share. Toyota always stays on the offensive looking for ways to be better than their competitors. Toyota wants to stay in front of its competitors and take advantage of any weaknesses they may show and capitalize on them to gain any advantage they can.

Grand strategies serve as the basis for achieving major long term objectives of a single business: concentration market, market development, product development, innovation, horizontal integration, vertical integration, joint venture, concentration diversification, conglomerate diversification, retrenchment, turnaround, divestiture and liquidation. Grand strategies are usually combined all strategies of the organization or company arena.

Figure—5.1 : Grand strategies Structures in enterprise's

Grand strategies Structures in enterprise's

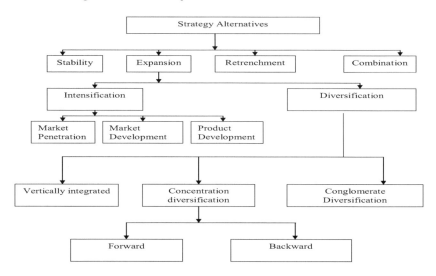

A grand strategy principally consists of stability strategies, expansion strategies, retrenchment strategies and combination strategies. These strategies are known as grand strategies or master strategies or direction strategies.

Features of Grand Strategies

The basic features of grand strategies are presented in the table:

Strategy	Basic Features
Stability	Stability strategy refers to maintaining the status quo of the existing business operation. Stability strategy aims at a slow growth rate It can be maintained the existing level of efforts in business. It is satisfied with incremental growth of its functional performance in terms of its customer groups, customer functions.

Expansion	An organization desired to expand extents its business network widening the scope of its customer groups, customer functions and state of the art technologies. Intensive expansion is a fundamental approach to safeguard and develop the organizations product market and thereby increased the volume of scales, profit, market share and total business network very rapidly. It can be entering new businesses that are unrelated to existing businesses.
Retrenchment	An organization decides to reduce its business operation by reducing the scope of customer groups or customer functions or alternative technologies with a view to have better control for better performance, retrenchment strategies are accepted. It can be dropped the business as such through sell out or liquidation.
Combination	Combination strategy refers to the combination of the stability, expansion and retrenchment strategy in different levels of the organization

CHARACTERISTICS AND SCOPE OF VARIOUS GRAND STRATEGIES

Stability Strategy

Stability strategy refers to maintaining the status quo of the existing business operation. Stability strategy aims at a slow growth rate. It follows as a matter of principle when an organization attempts incremental growth of its functional performance in terms of its customer groups, customer functions, and alternative technologies, whether in combination or individually. Thus when an organization decides to serve the same target customer groups with same products service and follows the same objective to maintain the stable business status, it can be termed as stability strategy. A company purely depends and run on continuing to serve the same clients by offering existing clients.

Characteristics of Stability Strategy

❖ A firm opting for a stability strategy maintains with the same business, same product-marked positions and functions, maintaining the same level of effort as at status quo of the existing business.

❖ It aims to enhance functional efficiencies in on achievement way, it is achieved through better deployment and utilization of resource.

❖ It involves the assessment of the firm which is maintaining the status quo in terms of desired income and profits.

❖ It can be helped to business to incremental improvements in functional efficiencies.

❖ Generally, this strategy will be quite modest in business growth objectives: it is applicable only companies which modest growth objective will vote for this strategy.

❖ This strategy is a safety oriented and status quo oriented strategy.

❖ It does not require much fresh investment.

❖ It is fairly frequently employed strategy in business.

❖ Companies which have followed this strategy, these companies are definitely expected benefits from concentrating its resource and attention towards the existing business/ products and markets.

❖ And the rewards are also limited in companies.

❖ Stability strategy does not permit the firm's renewal process for bringing in fresh investments and new products and markets for the firm.

EXPANSION STRATEGY

Samsung expansion strategy is to introduce a new version of Smartphone to across the globe and special concentration of emerging markets. Apple and Samsung are competing in the Smartphone global market. Both companies have gained competitive advantage but they spent large marketing budgets, extensive distribution channels and attractive product portfolios.

When an organization desired to expand extents its business network widening the scope of its customer groups, customer functions and state of the art technologies, companies have the making of an expansion strategy. Expansion or growth strategy is principally adopted when an organization enhances its level of objectives with high target. Intensive expansion is a fundamental approach to safeguard and develop the organizations product market and thereby increased the volume of scales, profit, market share and total business network very rapidly.

Apple introduced new product is iOS 7 and Smartphon 5c and 5s, it is a dramatic market expansion strategy and result in a major market expansion for Apple laptop and desktop products across the world. An Apple strategy admitting that both mobile and desktop devices from the company could run on the same processors. Apple has expanded into global markets, recording unprecedented levels of revenue and profit. In today's business environment a company has to stay ahead of the curve by being knowledgeable about changes in technology as well as continuing to find new ways to be competitive and meet customer demands.

Characteristics of Expansion Strategy

- ❖ Expansion strategy is just opposite to stability strategy.
- ❖ Expansion strategies are those strategies which are highly rewarded in companies and also the risk is too high in business.
- ❖ It is flexible and most frequently employed generic strategy.

❖ It is the true growth strategy; the company's aims of expansion business activities in this way to meet its growth objectives in firms.

❖ It involves the redefinition of the business activities of the company.

❖ It requires fresh investments and it involves the process of renewal of the company in this way introducing new business / products /markets are facilitated only by expansion strategy.

❖ It is highly versatile strategy: it offers several permutations and combinations for growth. For this purpose, the firm's opting for the expansion strategy can generate many alternatives within the strategy by altering its propositions regarding in terms of products, markets, functions and pick the one that suits it most.

❖ It has fold two major routes; intensification and diversification.

❖ Intensification and diversification are the tool of growth strategies; it pursues difference it's actually growth in business.

❖ Firm's intensification strategy pursues growth by working its current business operation in businesses.

❖ Intensification can be encompassed with the three alternative routes as outlined:

    a) Market penetration strategy
    b) Market development strategy
    c) Product development strategy

❖ Diversification strategy refers to the expansion of business into new businesses that are outside the current businesses and markets.

❖ An important type's diversification as listed below:

    Related diversification
    Unrelated diversification
    Internal diversification
    External diversification
    Horizontal diversification
    Vertical diversification

> Active diversification
> Passive diversification
> Concentric diversification

❖ Vertically integrated diversification involves that firm's are going into new businesses which are related to current ones.

❖ Vertical integration further classified into two broad components such as forward integration and backward integration.

❖ The firm's remain vertically within the given product process sequence: it is intermediaries in the chain become new businesses.

❖ Concentration diversification refers to introducing new products which are connected to the firm's existing process or technology. Therefore, the new products are not vertically linked to the existing ones. They are not considered as intermediates.

❖ They serve new functions in new markets and it is spinned off from the firm's existing facilities.

❖ Conglomerate diversification refers to a new business is added to the firm's portfolio. It is unrelated diversification and it disconnected from the existing business operation of firm's in the form of process / technology / function. In this strategy, there is no connection between the existing business and new business.

RETRENCHMENT/ DIVESTMENT STRATEGY

The growth of Samsung and Apple has continued to impact Nokia and finally Nokia acquired by Microsoft for promoting Windows phone. Nokia's Windows Phone Lumia version portfolio has improved significantly in recent months. Apple's major competitors are Google, Samsung, Microsoft, and Others.

When an organization decides to reduce its business operation by reducing the scope of customer groups or customer functions or alternative technologies with a view to have better control for better performance, retrenchment strategies are accepted. In retrenchment strategy, unattractive and unwanted areas of business are sequenced gradually. It is not a matter of failure of business planning, rather well planned exercise to get rid of unprofitable parts of a business which will help the organization concentrate its total attention on the most profitable and promising areas of business only.

Apple launched iTools. It offers consumer internet services which later became Mac, and eventually the infamously failed MobileMe. Apple launched Ping, is a social music service that also failed. These failed services provided essential learning and Apple's efforts reveals a long road of successes and more importantly failure that leads to success.

Characteristics of Retrenchment/ Divestment Strategy

❖ It involves retrenchment of some of the activities in a given business of the firm or sells out of some of the business assets.
❖ It is one of the corporate strategies to reduce its operation by reducing the scope of customer groups and customer functions.
❖ It involves the redefinition of the business operation.
❖ Compulsions in this strategy are different and vary in business operation.
❖ Retrenchment is necessary in the following firm's conditions:

> When business unprofitable
> When high competition from the competitor
> When an industry is over capacity
> When failure of strategy

COMBINATION STRATEGY

In changing business environment, an organization may also find it beneficial to adapt a unique combination of stability, expansion and retrenchment in different levels related areas of business which depending on the business environment. In other words, combination strategy refers to the combination of the stability, expansion and retrenchment strategy in different levels of the organization.

Apple combination strategies to expand its presence in global markets including, but not limited to foreign outsourcing and importing, exporting, foreign licensing, and foreign direct investment. Foreign outsourcing and importing provide production at cheaper costs which makes products.

Major Reasons for Organizations Adopting Different Grand Strategies

A firm's has adopted a stability strategy in the following conditions:

- ❖ It is less risk, it involves less change and people feel comfortable with things which are happening in firms.
- ❖ The business environment relatively stable condition.
- ❖ Expansion of business is threatening to firm's.
- ❖ Firm's consolidation required through stabilizing after a period of rapid expansion of business operation.

A firm's adopted Expansion strategy in the following conditions:

- ❖ It's imperative when the environment demands increase the pace of activity in a firm's operations.
- ❖ It is the results of expanding business operation in firms; chief executive is the responsible person for the firm's growth.
- ❖ Increase the size of business operation which is control over the market vis-a-vis competitors.
- ❖ It is advantageous to firm's in this way enhancing the scale of operations.

Firm's adopted Retrenchment strategy in the following conditions:

- ❖ When the management no longer wishes to remain in business both partly or wholly due to continuing losses and unviable.
- ❖ When business environment could be faced threaten to firm's operations.
- ❖ It can be ensured to be a reallocation of resources from unprofitable to profitable business.

Firm's Combination Strategy is adopted in the following conditions:

- ❖ An organization is large and ready to face complex environment in business operations.
- ❖ An organization is consisting of different businesses, each of which comes under the different industry that requiring a different response.

PRODUCT MARKET EXPANSION GRID

Newer tech genomes, such as Amazon and Google operate along similar lines. They are product driven companies and their strategy flows from that. They see a problem they can fix, attack it with fervor and then figure out what the business opportunity is.

Expansion or growth strategy can either be via intensification or diversification. Product market expansion grid developed by Igor Ansoff gave framework as presented that explained the intensification options available to a firm.

Figure—5.2 : Product Market Expansion Grid

Growth in existing product markets Increased market share Increased product usage Increase the frequency used Increase the quantity used Find a new application for current users	Product development Add product features, product refinement Develop a new generation product Develop new product for the same market
Market development Expand geographically Target new segments	Diversification involving new products and new markets Related Unrelated

Market Penetration

Market penetration strategy is the one most important expansion strategy of the current business. The firms direct its core resources to the profitable growth of a single product. It is in a single market and with a single technology.

Penetration of Strategy of Apple's focus for global expansion of emerging market for China, India, Brazil, etc.. India and China is an emerging market for Apple not only because of the cheap labor, but because it's a strong economy with the biggest population of the globe.

Market Development

Market development is consisting of marketing present's products and services which offered by company, company is required to be adding different channels of distribution or by changing the content of advertising or promotional media. IBM's Market Development

Strategies to increase Growth and Revenue Opportunities for Small and Medium Businesses in this way to gain market development and also provide financial assistance for technology upgradation to clients and sell its products and services and expand market operation.

Product development

It involves substantial modification of existing products and services or creation of new, but these are related items that can be marketed to current customers through established channels. A company developing the new products is becoming smarter in feature, using advanced technology, it is the result of innovation, well designed, and testing and attractive clients.

CHAPTER 6

DIVERSIFICATION

INTRODUCTION

Fortune 500 companies diversify their business operation in emerging market and Most of the fastest growing economies are in Africa and Central Asia. It results that a company gets attractive terrain market, faster growth for products and services, expects huge profitability and more stability in a business. A company will make diversification due to access physical assets and access to new and emerging markets, innovative technological skills and expertise supply channel, manufacturing and quality of products and services provides for ultimate clients and the establishment of a platform for diversification of business operating across the world.

Companies are adding new lines of business to get new customers and new market across the globe. For instance, the new diversification strategy of Apple with the companies that assemble its products, granting lower build costs and increased resilience to changing market conditions. Apple diversified product lines such as Macs, iPod, iPad, iPhones. Apple is busy in introducing new and innovative products to grab the attention of the customers. Diversification strategy Apple's ensure that to get more sales in the emerging markets, to create interesting and excited products, to give Android tough competition and to introduce smaller gadgets with high quality and low cost.

DIVERSIFICATION

It is a marketing strategy of a any company. It brings profitability, increase the sales. It is happening from a company introduce new products and services to new market and also existing market. A company diverse it business operation through merger, acquisition, internal start up, joint venture. These are pursued with the same technical, financial and merchandise resource used for the original product line. It usually require for a company to acquire new skills, new technologies and new facilities.

Diversification refers to a company is diverting the business focus from the existing traditional areas to new promising areas. Since technology is changing day by day, 'customer' demands are changing accordingly. The company introduced new and substitute products and service available in the market to meet the customer's expectations and to draw their attention. These changing attitudes of the customers, the company has opened more and more new areas of promising business. Diversification may involve internal or external, related or unrelated, horizontal or vertical, active or passive dimensions. The change of business focus may be either in terms of customer function, customer group and new alternative technologies.

TYPES OF DIVERSIFICATION

Successfully Diversification strategy of The Tata group. This group covers motor vehicles, cars, consulting, software, telecoms, information technology power, and steel, tea and coffee, chemicals and hotels. Tata Consultancy Services (TCS) is Asia's largest software company. Tata Steel is India's largest steelmaker and number ten in the world. Taj Hotels Resorts and Palaces are India's biggest luxury hotel group by far. Tata Power is the India's largest private electricity company. Tata Global Beverages is the world's second-largest maker of branded tea. Tata Tea's takeover of Tetley Group, a British company, Tata Steel bought Corus, Europe's second-largest steelmaker, Tata Motors paid $2.3 billion for Jaguar Land Rover (JLR). Tata Consultancy Services a leading IT services, consulting and business solutions firm completed the acquisition of ALTI SA, a France Company.

Samsung, Apple, Microsoft and Google companies have a successful diversification strategy to achieve long term goals.

A company is going to diversify its business operation. Company leaders or Strategic group enables to know the types of diversification will make for operation of business and its results and impact towards the corporate strategy of a company. A strategist knows the an important type's diversification and which type of diversification will be relevant to the business. Several diversification types are as listed below:

> Related diversification
> Unrelated diversification
> Internal diversification
> External diversification
> Horizontal diversification
> Vertical diversification
> Active diversification
> Passive diversification
> Concentric diversification
> Conglomerate diversification

RELATED DIVERSIFICATION

A company will go for related diversification when companies' businesses are said to be related when their value chains possess competitively valuable cross-business value chain matchups.

Related diversification is diversification into a new business activity that is linked to the company's existing business activity normally these activities are commonality between one or more components of each activity's of existing business activity of value chain. Normally these linkages are based on manufacturing marketing or technological commodities. Most companies favor related diversification strategies because of the performance enhancing potential of cross-business synergies.

Related diversification options for manufacturer in business as outlined:

❖ Exchange or Share assets or competencies, thereby exploiting the following:

- Brand name of company
- Marketing skills of company
- Sales and distribution capacity
- Manufacturing skills
- R&D and new product capability

❖ Economies of scale for company's products and services

Example of Related Diversification of **JOHNSON & JOHNSON** company. It offers Baby products, First-aid products, Medical devices, Surgical & Hospital products, Contact lenses and Personal Care products to customers across the globe.

Related diversification strategy of **GILLETTE** Blades and Razors Tooth Brush (Oral B) Toiletries products Hair dryers, Shavers.

Related diversification strategy of **PEPSICO** Soft drinks Fruit juices (Tropicana) Other beverages (Aquafina bottled water etc.,) Sports drinks (Gatorade) Snack foods (Lays, Chee—tos etc.,) Breakfast products

Related diversification strategy of **PROCTER & GAMBLE** Hair care products Household cleaning/care Beauty care products Laundry products

UNRELATED DIVERSIFICATION

Reliance Anil Dhirubhai Ambani Group successful unrelated diversification strategy. Telecom, Capital, Power, Infrastructure,

Entertainment and Health is the unrelated diversification of this group.

Unrelated diversification is diversification into a new business area that has no obvious connection with any of the companies existing areas. Unrelated diversification options for a manufacturer as outlined:

- ❖ Manage and allocate cash flow in the company
- ❖ Obtain high rate of investment in the company
- ❖ Obtain for bargain price
- ❖ Refocus a firm
- ❖ Reduce risk of operating in multiple product markets
- ❖ Tax benefits
- ❖ Obtain liquid assets in the company
- ❖ Vertical integration of company
- ❖ Defend against a takeover in firms.

Unrelated diversification strategy of **WIPRO.** Electrical appliances, Information Technology, Computer accessories Toilet soap (santoor), GE medical system, Baby care products is the unrelated diversification of WIPRO.

Unrelated diversification strategy of **LG.** Mobile Phones Television, Radio Projectors Home appliances, Lamps, Notebooks is the unrelated diversification of **LG.**

The unrelated diversification strategy of **TATA GROUPS.** Home appliances, Financial services, Watches, Telecom services, Information technology, Tea products is the unrelated diversification of **TATA GROUPS.**

Unrelated diversification strategy of **RELIANCE.** Telecom services, Power, Petro-chemical products, Mobile phones, Construction, Textiles, Mutual funds, money is the unrelated diversification of **RELIANCE.**

INTERNAL DIVERSIFICATION

One form of internal diversification is to market existing products in new markets. Apple introduces 5c and 5s iPhone to emerging markets like China, India, African countries. A company looking for existing products will be sold to new market and new customer at different location on the globe.

Diversification business activities within the company such is known as internal diversification. It means that a company ready to introduce new products in the same geographical areas. Another form of internal diversification is to market new products in existing markets. Generally this strategy involves using existing channels of distribution to market new products.

A company makes internal diversification when a company has conglomerate growth. This strategy would entail marketing new and unrelated products to new markets. This strategy is the least used among the internal diversification strategies due to most risky.

EXTERNAL DIVERSIFICATION

Mergers are one common form of external diversification. Mergers occur when two or more firms combine operations to form one corporation. Acquisitions are another form of external diversification, a second form of external growth, occur when the purchased corporation loses its identity. Acquisitions usually occur when a larger firm purchases a smaller company. Microsoft has acquired Nokia's mobile device business and licensing of patents for $7.2 billion. It is the example of the external diversification of business operation. Microsoft's purchase of Nokia's mobile phone business and reshuffle its business operation in emerging markets such as China and India.

External diversification involves to diversification of the business activities like manufacturing, products, marketing, technological changes diversified with the other companies to save for the operating costs of the goods and service.

HORIZONTAL DIVERSIFICATION

Horizontal diversification is undertaken in order to increase market share by expansion of the same product lines with more varieties to serve customers in different areas, of different types and affluence levels. Horizontal diversification may be taken up to expand business geographically into new territories by taking up an increase market share and improve business volume. Horizontal integration or diversification involves the firm moving into operations at the same stage of production.

VERTICAL DIVERSIFICATION

Apple product iPhone cannibalized iPod, iPad and also have cannibalized the MacBook. And expect the same sense of Microsoft product Windows did cannibalize DOS. Vertical integration occurs when firms undertake operations at different stages of production. Involvement in the different stages of production can be developed inside the company (internal diversification) or by acquiring another firm (external diversification). Vertical integration is usually related to existing operations and would be considered concentric diversification. Horizontal integration can be either a concentric or a conglomerate form of diversification.

Microsoft successful products primarily through internal development: DOS, Windows, Word, Excel, PowerPoint, Xbox by using vertical diversification. Vertical diversification means diversification into a new production line to produce items required as inputs for other main products of the same company. Vertical integration refers to company diversify its business into a number of different business areas. Diversification into a new production line to produce goods and service required as inputs for other main products of the same company. For instance a company diversifies its business into a number of different business areas like banking and financial services, energy and utility, health care and insurance, manufacturing retail, telecom. It may be undertaken by a company with the purpose of either maintaining continuous flow of products and service to customers. The Vertical Integration Company offers numerous products and service for satisfying customers. A company is opening its own sales and marketing division and showrooms for selling product and service to customer instead of selling through agents and distributors. It can be controlled over the input supply and output distribution also.

Samsung, a large technology conglomerate, has thrived by making everything from LCD panels to processors, televisions and Smartphones.

Vertical integration further classified into two broad categories. They are listed below:

- Backward or Upstream integration
- Forward or Downstream integration

Upstream or backward Integration

Jindal Steel and Power (JSPL) adopts a backward integration strategy securing raw materials and steers a remarkable turnaround making and made it the most valuable Indian steel company. Back integration or upstream refers to the company is diversifying the business operation towards some of the raw materials or input supply. Backward integration involves moving into intermediate manufacturing and raw material production. Backward integration allows the diversifying firm to exercise more control over the quality of the supplies being purchased. Backward integration also may be undertaken to provide a more dependable source of needed raw materials. Forward integration allows a manufacturing company to assure itself of an outlet for its products. Forward integration also allows a firm more control over how its products are sold and serviced. Furthermore, a company may be better able to differentiate its products from those of its competitors by forward integration. By opening its own retail outlets, a firm is often better able to control and train the personnel selling and servicing its equipment.

Downstream or Forward integration

Forward integration or downstream refers to the company is diversifying business operations for marketing sales distribution of products and services and taking up these activities to bring the organization closer to the ultimate customer.

Figure—6.1: Stages in the Raw material to Consumer Production Chain

Stages in the Raw material to Consumer Production Chain

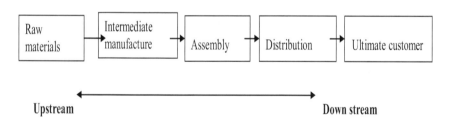

Table 6.1 highlights the stages in the raw material to customer production chain. It indicates the four steps are listed below:

❖ Intermediate manufacture
❖ Assembly
❖ Distribution
❖ Ultimate customer

Backward or Upstream integration

Backward integration involves moving into intermediate manufacturing and raw material production. Forward integration involves movement into distribution. At each stage in chain, value is added to the product. It means that a company at that stage takes the product produced in the previous stage, transforms it in some way and then sells the output at a higher price to a company at the next stage in the chain. The difference between the price paid for inputs and the price at which the product is sold is a measure of the value added at that stage.

A company achieve full integration what it produces all of a particular input needed for its possessor when it disposes of all of its inputs through its own operations.

Taper integration occurs when a company buys from independent suppliers in addition to company-owned suppliers or when it disposes of its output through independent outlets in addition to company owned outlets.

CREATING VALUE THROUGH VERTICAL INTEGRATION

Vertical integration dictates that one company controls the end product as well as its component parts. In technology, Apple for 35 years has championed a vertical model, which features an integrated hardware-and-software approach. For instance, the iPhone and iPad have hardware and software designed by Apple, which also designed its own processors for the devices. This integration has allowed Apple to set the pace for mobile computing. "Despite the benefits of specialization, it can make sense to have everything under one roof,"

A company pursuing vertical integration is normally motivated by a desire to strengthen the competitive position of its original or core business. There are four vital arguments for pursuing a vertical integration strategy. They are as listed below:

- ❖ Enables the company to build barriers to new competition
- ❖ Facilitates investments in efficiency-enhancing specialized assets.
- ❖ Protects product quality
- ❖ Results in improved scheduling

Enables the Company to Build Barriers to New Competition

The company's vertical integration backward to gain control over the source of inputs and distribution channels. A company can build effective distribution channels for distribution of products and service. The company builds barriers to new entry into its industry to extend to apply to this strategy effectively to avoid competition. Therefore, thereby enabling the company to charge a higher price and make greater profits.

Facilitating Investments in Specialized Assets

A specialized asset is an asset that is designed to perform a specific task and whose value is significantly reduced in its next best use. A specialized asset may be a piece of equipment or skills. The skills acquired by the companies or individuals through training and experience. Companies and individuals invest in specialized asset because these assets allow them to lower the costs of value creation and to better differentiate their product offering from that of competitors, thereby, facilitating premium pricing. These specialized assets use very specialized purposes. Companies always invest in specialized equipment because it enables it to lower its manufacturing costs and increase its quality. Secondly it invests in developing highly specialized technological knowledge because it develop better products than their rivals. Therefore, specialization can be achieved a competitive advantage at the industry level.

A company may find it very difficult to persuade other companies' in adjacent stages in the raw material to consumer production chain to undertake investments in specialized assets. As a result, companies or individuals are to realize the economic gains associated with investments. It may have to vertically integrate into such adjacent stages and make the investment itself.

Protecting Product Quality

The companies' main aim is protecting product quality. Vertical integration enables a company to become a differentiated player in its core business. If a company is the integration, therefore it can protect product quality without affecting standard ness of the product quality.

Improved Scheduling

Strategic advantages arise from the easier planning, coordination and scheduling of adjacent processes. It made possible in vertically integrated organizations or companies can be particularly important in companies trying to relate the benefits of just in time inventory systems.

DISADVANTAGES OF VERTICAL INTEGRATION

Cost Disadvantages

Cost is the main factor of the company to gain a production cost advantages. Meanwhile vertical integration can raise costs, if a company becomes committed to purchasing inputs from company owned suppliers when low cost external sources of supply exist.

Company owned might high operating costs compared with the independent suppliers.

Technological Changes

Technological changes are other disadvantages of the vertical integration. When technology changes fast and outdated its plants and equipment. Therefore, it is also major disadvantages of the company.

Demand Uncertainty

It can also be extremely risky in unstable or unpredicted demand condition. In this case, it is very difficult to achieve their activities in the company.

Others

Vertical integration poses problems of balancing capacity at each stage in the value chain.

Integrating forward or backward often calls for radically different skills and business capabilities.

Backward vertical integration into the production of parts and components can reduce a company's strength.

CONCENTRIC DIVERSIFICATION

Concentric diversification is to concentrate the direction of business for expansion and diversification is to concentrate the direction in the same and attendant product lines. Concentric diversification may take the form of marketing related or technology related diversification.

Active diversification is the long-term expansion of the business activities. Passive diversification is the short term and negative impact of continuity of long term contracts with partners.

- ❖ The concentration diversification, the business is linked to the company existing business through its process, technology and marketing.
- ❖ The new product is only connected in a loop like manner at one or more points in the company's existing process or technology or product chain.

CONGLOMERATE DIVERSIFICATION

Microsoft acquired mobile device maker Nokia mobility and will soon manufacture Smartphone and windows phone. Google recently acquired mobile-device maker Motorola Mobility and will soon manufacture smart phones and television set-top boxes. Amazon's Kindle Fire tablet represents its bridge between hardware and e-commerce. Oracle bought Sun Microsystems and now champions engineered systems (integrated hardware-and-software devices). And even long-standing software giant Microsoft now makes hardware for its Xbox gaming system. Technology titans are increasingly looking like vertically integrated conglomerates largely in an attempt to emulate the success of Apple.

It refers to the new businesses or products are disjoint from the existing businesses or products in every way;

- ❖ It is a totally unrelated diversification.
- ❖ In process or technology or function, these are no connection between the new products and the existing ones.
- ❖ It is no common thread at all with the company's present position.

Creating Value through Diversification

Most companies first consider diversification when they are generating financial resources, therefore, it is excess to maintain to competitive advantage in their original or core business. The diversified company can generate value in three main routes. They are listed below:

- ❖ Acquiring and restructuring
- ❖ Transferring competencies
- ❖ Economies of scope

ACQUIRING AND RESTRUCTURING

Acquiring and restructuring involved with acquiring and restructuring poorly run enterprises. A restructuring strategy rests on the presumption that an efficiently managed company can create value by acquiring inefficient and poorly managed enterprises and improving their efficiency. This approach can be considered diversification because the acquired company does not have to be in the same industry as the acquiring company for the strategy to work. Improvements in the efficiency of an acquired company can come from a number of sources. They are listed below:

The acquiring company usually replaces the top management team of the acquired company with more aggressive top management team.

The new top management team is encouraged to sell off any unproductive assets like executive's jets and elaborate corporate head quarters and to reduce staffing levels.

The new top management team is also encouraged to intervene in the running of the acquired business to seek out routes of improving the unit's efficiency, quality, innovativeness, and customer responsiveness.

To motivate the new top management team and other employees of the acquired unit undertake such actions, increases in their pay may be linked to industries in the performance of the acquired unit. The acquiring company often establishes performance goals for the acquired company. Strategic Acquisition targets are listed below:

- ❖ Enabled by powerful cash generated
- ❖ Able to leverage company's global infrastructure
- ❖ General product-like highly scalable in growth areas
- ❖ A form of new product development

Transferring Competencies

The company's diversification strategy of transferring competencies seek out new business related to their existing business by one or more value creation functions, for instance, manufacturing, marketing, materials management and R&D. They want to create value by drawing on the distinctive skills in one or more of their existing value creation function in order to improve the competitive position of the new business. It can improve the efficiency of their existing business.

Economies of Scope

It arises when two or more business units share resources like;

- ❖ Manufacturing facilities
- ❖ Distribution channels
- ❖ Advertising
- ❖ R&D costs
- ❖ Each business unit utilized their capacity better and reduced to operating cost.

RETRENCHMENT, DIVESTMENT AND LIQUIDATION STRATEGY

Wal-Mart is the biggest retailer in the world, with sales of $135 billion in 26 countries outside the U.S. It decided to retrenchment of retail operation association with its Indian partner, Bharti Enterprises.

When an organization decides to reduce its business operation by reducing the scope of customer groups or customer functions or alternative technologies with a view to have better control for better performance, retrenchment strategies are accepted. In retrenchment strategy, unattractive and unwanted areas of business are sequenced gradually. It is not a matter of failure of business planning, rather well planned exercise to get rid of unprofitable parts of a business which will help the organization concentrate its total attention on the most profitable and promising areas of business only.

- ❖ These things are done through an attempt to find out the problem areas and diagnose the causes of the company's problems.
- ❖ Once identified the problems, firms will be taken the next steps to solve the problems.
- ❖ This result is to search different type's retrenchment strategies in businesses.
- ❖ For retrenchment process, a firm will be selected and adopted at turnaround strategy.
- ❖ And also adapt to the divestment strategy to reduce functional activities in firms.
- ❖ If none of these actions cannot be worked, that time a firm can be chosen to abandon the activities totally in terms of liquidation strategy.

TURNAROUND STRATEGY

Alcatel-Lucent Planning to cut 10,000 positions—roughly 14 percent of its workforce. It will happen shortly, as the telecom equipment maker tries to speed up its turnaround. Many companies restructure their operations divesting themselves of their diversified activities, because they wish to focus more their core business area. An integral part of the restructuring, therefore, it is the development of strategy for turning around the company's core or remaining business areas.

In this section, we shall review in some detail the various steps to be taken by companies in turnaround troubled business areas. We shall first look at the causes of corporate decline and then discuss the main elements of successful turnaround strategies.

❖ Retrenchment can be done either internally or externally in the company. Internal retrenchment which takes into place that is emphasis to lay on improving its internal efficiency which is known as a turnaround strategy.

There are certain conditions or indicators are the main reasons for turnaround is needed to company's have to survival, growth, development and increased profitability. The major danger signs in the industry are listed below:

❖ Persistent negative cash flow in business
❖ Negative profits in business
❖ Declining market shares of firm's
❖ Deterioration in physical facilities in business.
❖ Over manning, high turnover of employees and low morale of human resource in company's.
❖ Uncompetitive products and services in industry.
❖ Mismanagement is the main reason in the company.

The Causes of Corporate Decline

Corporate decline due to several factors are directly or indirectly linked with the performance of the company. Causes are the impact of the corporate declines as listed below:

- ❖ Poor management
- ❖ Over expansion
- ❖ Inadequate financial controls
- ❖ High costs
- ❖ New competition
- ❖ Unforeseen demand shifts
- ❖ Organizational inertia

Poor Management

Poor management involves a multitude of sins; it is ringing from sheer incompetence to neglect of core businesses and an insufficient number of good managers. Therefore, these things are not necessarily a bad thing. Research study showed that in the presence of a dominant and an autocratic chief executive with a passion for empire building strategies characterizes involved for many failing companies. It happens due to Miserable employees, a big ego, low productivity, resistance to change, and a one-way communication style are often signs of bad management skills.

Over Expansion

Rapid expansion and extensive diversification, these diversifications tend to be poorly conceived and adds little value to a company much diversification its result is loss of control and inability to cope with recessionary conditions. Moreover, companies expand rapidly their business involves large amounts of debt financing. Adverse economic conditions can limit a company's ability to meet its debt requirements and can participate a financial crisis.

Inadequate financial controls

It is the common trend of the business. Financial manager is a failure to assign profit responsibility for the financial consequences of their actions, it can encourage to mid level managers to employ excess staff and spend resource beyond what is necessary for maximum efficiency of the company.

High Costs

Inadequate financial control can lead to high costs. Its common cause like low labor productivity and management has failed to introduce new labor saving technologies and high rate of wages for employees. These are an important factor for companies competing on costs in the global market and have a failure to realize economies of scale, therefore, it result impact on companies low market share.

New Competition

Apple also faces heightened competition from Smartphone maker Samsung, Microsoft, and Google. New competition is essential to companies for competition in the industrial world. A company ready to tackle competition from rivals. Because of new technology made huge cutthroat competition and increase in productivity at low cost of output. Many companies have failed because of unable to face threats of competitors. Therefore, new competition kills idle companies in the business world.

Unforeseen Demand Shifts

Environment threat like marketing, technology, political, social, legal, cultural environment can change open market opportunities for new products. Its consequence is the unforeseen demand shifts from old to new products. Therefore, the customer has preference to buy new product at a low cost. When companies fail to fulfillment of the above fact then have a failure in the business world.

Organizational Inertia

The emergence of powerful new competition and unforeseen shifts in demand might not be enough to cause corporate decline. Organization is slow to respond to environmental changes. Nokia phone sales plummet across the globe: it results that it acquired by Microsoft.

MAIN ELEMENTS OF SUCCESSFUL TURNAROUND STRATEGIES

There are essential elements of every company's turnaround business plan. The two most important sections are the Executive Summary of problem areas, the solution, market size, revenue stream, competition, marketing strategy, sales strategy, client retention, management and capital and the Financial Forecast and the turnaround plan include the elements: Target Market, Marketing Plan, Sales Plan, Competitive Analysis, Employee Retention Plan, Client Retention Plan, Operating Plan. Main Elements of Successful turnaround strategies are as follows

- ❖ Changing leadership
- ❖ Redefining strategic focus
- ❖ Asset sales and closures
- ❖ Improving profitability
- ❖ Acquisitions

Changing the Leadership

Old leadership had failure, new leader is an essential element of retrenchment and turnaround situation to resolve the crisis, to motivate lower level managers, listen to the views of others and delegate power when appropriate.

Redefining Strategic Focus

It refers to redefining company's strategy for restructuring of business. It is identifying the business in the portfolio which has the best for the company for long-term profit and growth prospectus and concentrating investment there.

Assets Sales and Closures

Having redefined its strategic focus, a company should divest as many unwanted assets as it can find buyer for and liquidate whatever remains. It is important not to confuse unwanted assets within profitable assets.

Improving Profitability

Improving profitability involves a number of steps to improve efficiency, quality, innovation and customer responsiveness. It involves the following issues:

- ❖ Layoffs white and blue collar employee
- ❖ Investments in labor saving equipment
- ❖ Assessment of profit, it is responsibility to individuals and subunits within the company, by a change of organizational structure if necessary.
- ❖ Tightening financial controls
- ❖ Cutting back on marginal products
- ❖ Reengineering business process to cut costs and boost productivity and
- ❖ Introducing total quality management

ACQUISITIONS

Google has acquired over 100 companies, with its largest acquisition being the purchase of Motorola Mobility, a mobile device manufacturing company. Turnaround strategy involves making an acquisition primarily to strengthen the competitive position of a company's remaining core operations.

Issues For Successful Turnaround Strategies

Apple, Microsoft, Google, Tata group, Reliance group, Mahindra group is successful turnaround strategies to enhance to new markets, new customers, new technology, and new products etc.,.

Turnaround strategies are to be successful because of successful issues which are related to firm's imperative focus on the short-term and long term financing needs as well as strategic issues which are suitable to make a workable action plan for a turnaround with companies are listed below:

- ❖ Analysis of product, market, production processes, competition and each market segment positioning.
- ❖ Strategic manager clear thinking about the marketplace and production logic.
- ❖ Proper implementation of plans of target setting, and get feedback and take right remedial action.

Contributory Elements for Turnaround in Firm's

- ❖ Changes in top level management in business
- ❖ Initial credibility building actions in firm's
- ❖ Neutralizing external pressures
- ❖ Initial control
- ❖ Identifying quick payoff activities
- ❖ Quick cost reductions

- ❖ Revenue Generations
- ❖ Asset liquidation for generating cash
- ❖ Mobilizations of the organizations
- ❖ Better internal coordination

DIVESTMENT/CUTBACK STRATEGY

It involves the sale and disposing off or shedding business units or product divisions or segments of business operations to reinvest the resources for other production and potential business purposes.

- ❖ Divestment is usually a part of revival, rehabilitation and restructuring plan attempted when a turnaround strategy becomes unsuccessful.
- ❖ The strategy in the case may be to sell off a part of business or products, or giving up the control over a subsidiary or a demerger so that the wholly owned subsidiaries may be floated off as an independent organization.
- ❖ Organization maybe choose to divest in two ways: a part of the organization may choose to divest by way of serving its financial and managerial control and separating it as an independent organization for all purposes. Alternatively, an organization may sell a unit outright for which marketing strategy should be proven.
- ❖ The basic objective underlying organization unit may be hindrance on the total profitability and growth, particularly when opportunities of strategic alternative investment exist. So, divestment may be a sensible positive strategic decision and not due to helpless condition. Further there may be other types of strategies like business level strategy, functional level strategy, annual strategy, grand strategy, and corporate strategy.

Reasons to Adopt Divestment Strategy in Firms

- ❖ A business had been acquired which proves that to be mismatched and cannot be integrated within the company.

❖ Persistent financial problems which create the negative cash flows from a particular business operation in the company which is to be needed for divestment of that business.

❖ Firm unable to cope to severity of competition from rival companies: it may cause to divest business operations.

❖ Technology up gradation is required, in this case, the firm able to survive but where it is possible for the firm to invest in it, a firm preferable option would be taken for divest business operations.

❖ A better alternative which may be available for investment that causing a firm to divest a part of its unprofitable businesses in the company's operations.

Liquidation Strategies

❖ Retrenchment strategy is considered the most and extreme and unattractive is liquidation strategy: it involves closing down a firm and selling its assets.

❖ It is considered as the last resort because which leads to serious consequences like loss of employment of workers and other employees, termination of opportunities where a company can pursue any future activities and the stigma of failure.

❖ In India, many small firms like small scale units, proprietorship firms and partnership ventures are liquidated frequently but medium and large sized companies rarely liquidate in India.

❖ The company management, government, banks and financial institutions, trade unions, suppliers and creditors and other agencies are extremely reluctant to take decisions or ask or formulate suitable policy for liquidation.

❖ Selling assets for implementing a liquidation strategy, it will be difficult to sell and difficult to find buyers for assets of liquidation firm. In this case, the liquidation company cannot be expected adequate compensation from the selling assets which as treated scrap by buyers.

Liquidation—the Strategy of Last Resort

Sometimes a business crisis is too far gone to salvage or is not worth salvaging given the resources it will take and its profit prospects. Closing a crisis-ridden business down and liquidating its assets is sometimes the best and wisest strategy of all strategic alternatives. Liquidation is the most unpleasant and painful because of the hardships of job eliminations and the effect of business closings in local communities. Therefore, in hopeless situations, an early liquidation effort usually serves owner-stock holder interests better than an inevitable bankruptcy.

End Game Strategies

End game strategy steers a middle course between pressuring the status quo and existing as soon as possible.

An end game strategy is a reasonable strategic option for a weak business in the following circumstances:

- When the industry's long-term prospects are attractive.
- When rejuvenating the business would be too costly or at best marginally profitable.
- When the firm's market share is becoming costly to maintain or defend.
- When reduced levels of competitive effort will not trigger an immediate or rapid falloff in sales.
- When the enterprise can redeploy the freed resources in higher opportunity areas.
- When the business is not a crucial or core component of a diversified company's overall lineup business
- When the business does not contribute other desired features to a company's business portfolio.